# Emotional Intelligence for Entrepreneurs

*How to Use the Secrets of Emotional Intelligence to Achieve Better Sales, Increase EQ, Improve Leadership, and Skyrocket the Profits of Your Business*

**Joel E. Winston**

By reading this document, the reader agrees that under no circumstances is the author responsible for any losses, direct or indirect, which are incurred as a result of the use of information contained within this document, including, but not limited to, — errors, omissions, or inaccuracies.

**Hello fellow Entrepreneur,**

This is what a high level of Emotional Intelligence means for you as a successful entrepreneur:

- More profitable negotiation skills
- Decision making based sound logic instead of on emotions
- Smoother communication

Which means better personal results and **higher profits in your business.**

So, don´t wait longer to receive ´The 30-Day Emotional Intelligence Booster Program´ by typing the link below:

https://joelewinston.com/eq-for-entrepreneurs-booster-program

**Or scan the below QR code** with your mobile.

Print the document and put it in visible place, so you can improve your Emotional Intelligence daily.

Now, it's time to **10X your business** and start reading....

Enjoy,

Joel

# Table of Contents

# Introduction

Starting a business is an exciting adventure. Once you first thought of the idea, you probably felt a thrill at the exciting things to come. Maybe you already tried a business and it didn't succeed like you wanted it to. Perhaps you picked it back up or started a new one with a fresh vision.

Maybe you do not have a business yet at all. Perhaps you are thriving, or maybe you need help to lift your business off the ground. No matter where you are in your entrepreneurialism, there is always more information to be learned that can really help drive your business to success. One of the best ways to ensure your business is running smoothly is to attune your emotional intelligence abilities and understand how we react and interact based on our levels of EQ.

This book is for ambitious entrepreneurs who want growth and to get better results with less effort. Sometimes it can be so draining to desperately try to make sales. Perhaps you have done some things you wish you didn't have to do, or maybe you pushed yourself past your limit on occasion, all in the name to make a sale. Maybe you see exactly what needs to be done, but you have trouble interacting with your employees. Whatever the problem might be, there's a good chance that an improvement of your emotional intelligence can help grow your business.

You can do this by understanding how to handle your team better as well. Though you are the backbone of your company and the ideas and visions that drive your business started with you, at this point, you have to realize the importance of your team as well. If we aren't conscious of how we can better lift our team up and work with them rather than against them, then our business will never succeed.

Aside from just working with our team, we also have to be aware of how we can better work with prospective clients and investors. We need the support of more than just ourselves and the people that are working for us. We need the inspiration from those that are a part of closing the sales after all!

One great book that helped inspire some of my greatest ideas around entrepreneurialism and emotional intelligence comes from Daniel Goleman's famous book, Emotional Intelligence. This book is enlightening for how emotions in our life can really drive our actions. Your emotions are part of you that can either help drive you forward or they can hinder your ability to properly operate throughout this life.

The first two chapters are going to focus on the ideas of his like these and all the other great psychological findings needed for the basic understanding of who we are, as well as the psychology needed to understand in others. The third and fourth chapters will be all about how you can start to apply these ideas and findings in your life, including important emotional intelligence models that outline approach and response.

You will find that you can better handle other demanding clients, sub-contractors, business partners, and shareholders when you increase your EQ levels. Most of the time, the way that we respond starts first with the basic emotion we feel. When we might sense attitude or animosity from someone else, it can either cause us to get defensive or perhaps our apprehension shows to the other prospect. This can be a turn-off or at least, start a power struggle in which we are destined to lose. Your emotions do not have to be a power-play and a struggle between competitors anymore. There are plenty of healthy ways that problems can be worked through, no matter how challenging they might feel initially.

Your working relationships will improve. You will find it easier to get what you want from others, while also having the emotional ability to stand up and say what you think is fair in any given setting. You will know how to ask for what you want and receive it in a way that is beneficial not just for you, but for the business overall.

Generally, this book is going to help you be more effective and productive by analyzing people. You will better understand how body language and facial movement can give you insight into what other people might be thinking, the way that their minds might be working.

You will learn how to use social skills in the work setting. The better your social skills are, the easier to becomes to actually drive sales. The easier it is to make sales, the faster the money comes in! This is not just good for you, but for your team. More profit means higher pay for your workers and better amenities for the business. Your clients will become more satisfied with this higher quality of work, only driving sales further.

We are going to discuss using the right emotions at the right time. There are times when you might need to really show your emotions and others where you have to remain as professional as possible.

This can lead to better deals with partners, clients, subcontractors, and shareholders while reducing stress. People will trust you more and at the end of the day, relationship management is most important. When your stress levels are lower, it will show and it can help people be more trusting of you and the things you might be asking.

The main focus is going to be self-awareness, self-regulation, social awareness, social skills, and assertiveness to become more productive, become a better entrepreneur, and to get more done with less energy and time.

Success is less determined by IQ and is more determined by EQ. The importance is self-awareness and social-awareness. Statistics show that the influence of IQ as well as EQ, in careers and working relationships is incredibly important for you and your employee's success.

To understand emotional intelligence, you should understand that there are some notable research and publications on the subject that are worthy of mentioning. We will dive further into this at the beginning of the book as well.

The first part of this book is an explanation of what EQ is. The better you can understand this, the easier it will be for you to constantly improve on it. The second part, we are going to give you practical steps to help improve your levels. We set it up in a thirty-day challenge so within a month's time, you will already be able to see the ways that you can improve your company all on your own.

# Part 1: Understanding the Foundation

## Chapter 1 – Human Emotions

Everyone has emotions, feelings, ideas, thoughts, and opinions. We all have a range of emotions that help to define who we are. Emotions come more naturally to us than most other aspects of our life. We do not always need to be taught how to feel certain things. When you stub your toe, you feel hurt. When you slip and fall, you can feel embarrassed, when you lose something or someone, you feel grief. There are many emotions that come very naturally to us. In the same breath, we certainly learn how to feel other emotions. You might feel guilty, but would you still feel that same guilt had someone not told you that you should? You might feel ashamed, but is that just because someone told you that you needed to feel this way?

Emotions are what separate us from each other and they separate us from animals as well. We all react differently to various stimuli, so we can't always be sure that one moment would have the same emotional reaction for everyone. Your emotions can be learned but they can also be inherent to your personality.

Many emotional responses are the same. When you see someone trip and fall, everyone might become concerned. You might hear a loud "Oh!" when others see someone trip and really smack their face or knees into the concrete. After that initial "oh!" you might see a branch in the kinds of emotional reactions.

Some people might laugh, thinking that the fall was no big deal. Others might stop and ask if everything is OK, becoming concerned that even though the person who fell says they are fine, there might be something else wrong. And then there are those people that would just keep walking if they saw someone fall and go on with their day as if they hadn't seen anything at all.

Your facial expressions can be the first sign of your emotions. Have you ever been studying something hard just to find that your face was sore from being scrunched up? Maybe you are excited and watching something amusing, your face in a gentle smile in anticipation. Perhaps someone is giving you a ton of attention and love, and you can't help but smile hugely. Maybe someone is making you mad, telling you a story that's a blatant lie, your face is confused and annoyed.

Our emotions can cause us greater feelings that extend beyond that initial reaction. Maybe you hear that a friend is newly engaged, your mood might end up being more excited for the rest of the day. Perhaps you woke up and read something in the news that angered you right away and the rest of your day is met with an inability to concentrate and general concern over the world. These simple reactions can be stretched out, all based on our emotional intelligence.

Our emotions can destroy us. A small hint of jealousy could turn into endless stalking to the point that you could violate someone's privacy. Perhaps a tiny fear over losing a job means constant stress and anxiety for the next three months as one tries to perform their job to the best of their abilities. Anger over something that happened in the past can stew into hatred that blinds us and controls the decisions we try and make.

They can inspire us to do something. Maybe you are sick of being broke, feeling the intense emotional turmoil, stress, and anxiety of your finances. This could inspire you to go back to school to get a higher degree and a better paying job. Perhaps you are feeling angry about the injustices for a certain group of people, so you spend your time devoted to fighting for their rights. Emotion has inspired some of the greatest people in the world to live out their dreams, in turn, inspiring more to try and achieve theirs.

They can also keep us held back out of fear. How many times have you stayed home from an event because you were scared? How many times did you stay quiet when you should have spoken up? The more that we start to understand what our emotions actually are, the easier it will be to find methods to manage them.

## Basic Human Emotions

At the root of all your emotions are your basic emotions. Whatever it is that you might be feeling can be traced back to just a select few kinds of emotions. Whether there are two, four, six, or twenty-seven is all up for debate. There's no manual for what it means to be human, so most scientists are just theorizing what the basic makeup of human emotions might be. We might never fully understand what they mean exactly, but we can determine what it means to feel them.

These emotions can seem like they hold the majority of the power over who we are. Your emotions have probably taken the driver's wheel on more occasions than you'd like to admit. Maybe you threw something when it wasn't working. Perhaps you texted an ex-girl- or boy-friend you didn't want to talk to. Maybe you slapped a friend, skipped an event, broke a glass, threw up, cried, spit, and did whatever other unpleasant, unattractive thing it was that left you with yet another emotion – guilt, shame, regret.

If there is one thing that we do hold reign over in our lives, we can be certain that it is our emotional reactions. You will not always be able to control the way you initially feel. If someone makes a joke about your appearance, maybe you feel hurt. After a moment of reflection, you realize it was just a distasteful joke made out of poor judgment, but that initial gut reaction of hurt is not something that's always within our control.

What you do have; however, is control over your reaction. When that person said something mean to you – you could have reacted by saying something mean back. Or you could have reacted with a laugh. That hurt was still there, but it is the emotional reaction that differs.

In order to really become an emotional expert, one must first ensure that they fully grasp what emotions are. You have to learn to separate the emotion from the reaction. Some people will say, "I couldn't help it! I was mad!" but that's no excuse. You are not at fault for how intensely you even feel an emotion, but it is still your responsibility as a human in a certain society to get a grip on the things that you feel.

When you have the ability to hold reign over these emotions, it will help you to become a more influential person. No longer will you be ruled by them. Others will see your willpower and admire the strength you have over the things that you feel.

Think of your basic emotions like colors. Yellow, red, blue, white, and black. These are the most basic building blocks of the color wheel. You can't have anything else without these fundamental pieces. Green, orange, purple... these colors are just combinations of the others. We will discuss the combined colors in a later section but for now, let's look deep at what these basic emotions are.

There are six common basic emotions referred to by a psychologist named Paul Eckman. These were happiness, sadness, anger, disgust, fear, and surprise. Since then, much other research has been done and many will narrow them down to four basic emotions, with as many as 27 others to be picked up from facial recognition. For the sake of this book, we'll refer to four and from there, expand into the advanced combination of emotions (Cherry, 2019).

### *Happiness*

The first emotion, the one that we all really strive for the most at the end of the day, is happiness. This is one of the best feelings in the world. When you have everything you need, you are happy. When you get what you want, you are happy. When you have an unexpected positive surprise, you are happy. When the opposite of any of these things happen, guess what? You're not happy.

When you are happy, you are feeling whole. There is not anything else that is required to make you feel more fulfilled. You are satisfied and living in the moment. You might understand there is not perfection present, but that doesn't stop you from being happy in the moment. You are distracted when you are happy. Maybe you are laughing at a funny joke or a TV show. Perhaps you are dancing with friends at a party.

You are in that moment, happy with who you are and what's around you.

Happiness is usually shown through smiles. Though some people might laugh when they are feeling manic or delusional, laughter most of the time indicates someone is having fun. Happy smiles indicate that the other person is satisfied. It is a little assurance that you didn't do anything wrong. Once you start to dive deeper into what kind of smile is being flashed – that's when you might start to discover that there is a deeper meaning to this smile.

When we are happy, we are relaxed. We lack fear, and any fear we do have might be positive excitement. We might be scared, but our excitement for the good that is to come outweighs any other negative things we might be feeling.

Happiness is something we measure as well. We might look at the people and the things around us and use this as a scale for whether or not our lives carry joy. Perhaps you are happy based on the things that you have; the number of cars, houses, and bags you own. Perhaps you are happy because you have so many amazing people in your life, a positive support system. It doesn't take a lot to be happy but when happiness is not present, it can take a lot out of you.

## *Sadness*

Sadness is the emotion that we try to avoid the most. Really, if you think about it, these two emotions can be the most basic. When you are experiencing good emotions, you'll automatically be happy; and when you are not, you might be in a state of sorrow. We shouldn't look at our emotions this stripped down; however, as they are so much more complex than that. However, it does help to make the comparisons between different states of emotion, as it will help you better see the way that these emotions can influence behavior and overall mood.

When we are feeling sad, it is hard to get anything done. We are distracted by the thing that happened. We might be going over and over in our heads everything that we wish we would have done differently. Even if you are sad about not having any money now, you might think back to two years ago when you purchased a $300 pair of shoes you only wore once. When you are sad, you are thinking about how other people are happy. It might make you even more sad to imagine the amount of happiness that you are not experiencing.

We are usually focused on finding a solution to make us feel better in order to bring ourselves out of the sadness. When you are sad, you might be thinking of what is needed in your life to make you feel better. However, we can sometimes be too consumed with our sadness to even have the strength to do anything about it.

We often forget what it is like to be happy at all when we're sad. We wonder if we are going to stay that way forever. We might be happy all day, but then that one moment of sadness sours every other good thing that we felt.

It can be easy to inflate sadness over happiness because we imagine that sad is not a place that we are supposed to be. We think that happiness is normal, that this is how things should always be. In reality, we should find an easy balance in the middle – a place of content. This is not how life will always be, but we have to learn to embrace this one basic emotion or else our entire lives will just be a fight against it.

Sometimes, we are even feeling sad on the inside but will try desperately to show that we are really living life in a happy way. Since feeling sad can be so challenging, we assume that it is something bad, something we need to hide. We pretend we're not sad, but so does everyone else, making it even harder to talk about the real things that we're feeling.

## *Fear and Surprise*

Both fear and surprise can sometimes go hand in hand. You might fear that your spouse is cheating on you, and still be surprised when you walk into the bedroom to see them with another lover. Perhaps you are fearful that you are going to get kicked out of your apartment, but you are still surprised to see the letter of eviction taped to your door.

Fear is usually a feeling to an unexpected circumstance and surprise is that reaction. When we are feeling both fear and surprise, we can sometimes react in the same way. The initial reaction doesn't always mean that we are showing our real feelings. As we go throughout life, we create certain expectations as a means of survival.

You expect that tomorrow you'll wake up again to your alarm, and then get ready for work, go to work, come home, and repeat. You have these expectations so that you are prepared to do what you have to do. When those expectations are not met, it can cause an emotion in us – fear or surprise. Fear is also something that we might experience beforehand. This is where surprise becomes the opposite to fear. When you are anxiously anticipating a big speech, maybe a surgery, or the arrival of a new baby, you might be fearful. You will be scared of everything that can go wrong.

For some, surprise could still elicit this reaction, especially if they consistently have negative perspectives and frequent pessimistic attitudes. Have you ever seen one of those makeover shows where the person is completely unhappy with the makeover? They knew it was happening, yet they were still reacting with negative shock, likely because they just do not as easily adjust to change as some others might.

Fear can quickly transform into surprise, and vice versa. For example, a mother might show fear in her surprised reaction at her 21-year-old daughter announcing her engagement to a man she dislikes. She might show that she's angry because the surprise didn't give her time to emotionally react. In time, she accepts her daughter's decision, changing her emotional reaction. Another mother might meet this daughter with intense surprise and an overall happy feeling. However, she might find out the wedding is only happening because the daughter is pregnant and the groom doesn't have a job either. Her surprise suddenly turns to fear as she has time to emotionally adjust to the situation. It's important to understand how fear and surprise, two things seemingly so different, can also be incredibly similar.

Fear doesn't have to be bad all the time either. We are fearful of spiders, but we might seek out watching spider movies because they thrill us. We can fear heights, but the surprise drop of a roller coaster is something that we still seek out. It is an adrenaline rush, an unexpected sensation, and a shockingly good feeling when it is felt in a controlled environment.

When we are startled, we are surprised, and we can also be fearful. It's really the situation that would depend on if it is something good or bad, whether your scare made you laugh or cry.

## Anger and Disgust

Anger is another emotion that can be defined as one of the most basic we have, along with feelings of disgust. Anger seems to come just as naturally as fear, happiness, and sadness. Toddlers can show their anger when something is taken away from them. They might also show their anger through hitting, kicking, and screaming. As we become teenagers, we can start to feel that anger directed inwards. We can quickly become self-loathing when we might have anger we do not know how to express. Rather than hating others it can become easier, and eventually more comfortable, to hate ourselves.

Anger comes when we are feeling as though something is not fair. We grow angry when things do not go our way. We might get angry at someone that gets more than us. Maybe we get angry when someone else gets their way and our opinions are forgotten.

Anger can be a result of us feeling threatened like something might be taken away. If you are afraid that someone is trying to take your position at work, perhaps you grow angry because you think that another person is taking the job from you. Anger can also be linked to sadness or fear if you really connect it as well. You might be sad that someone hurt your little brother, so you are angry with their bully. It can be a secondary emotion to one that is felt more basically. It is still an emotion that will help to drive others in a different direction.

When we're angry, then we can often show other signs and symptoms of disgust. We might feel like a person is using repulsive behavior. They might be acting in a way that we never would, and we end up thinking they are terrible people for choosing to do the things they do.

We might not see the use of something. We might be disgusted at the idea of someone using a leash on their child because we do not understand why anyone would want to do that. We might grow disgusted at those who spew hate and bullying online because we do not understand why they feel the need to be so detestable.

We can be disgusted when we do not understand. Those people that do spew the hate and partake in cyberbullying might be disgusted at their victims because they do not understand the challenges that others face. When only one side of a story is understood, it can be easy to grow disgusted as we do not fully grasp what it means to be on the other side.

You are simply disgusted at things that are bad for you. Have you ever seen a cat walk up to a bug on the ground, sniff it, and walk away? They could have eaten it, but they were able to see it wasn't good for them and walked away. We have similar reactions to other stimuli. We might see that it is not for us, so we go to the extreme and think that it is disgusting, based around our opinion.

## Advanced Combination Emotions

Your combination emotions are what results as a mixture of the basic emotions. In reference to the color comparison in the last section, think of your combination emotions as the more complex colors like green, purple, and orange. These only exist because of a combination of other emotions. Then you add in some white or black, and those emotions can start to get more positive or negative as well.

Perhaps you have a pretty green color and you splash some more yellow in to make it lime. You could also splash some blue into that to bring it back to a neutral green. Then throw in some black and you start to get a forest green.

Can you see how one emotion can greatly affect a combination of two other emotions that have already been blended? This is where our personalities start to form. We can pick up different traits based on consistent emotions that we've felt in the past.

All of these complex emotions can really boil down to the basic ones, but if we want to really understand how to feel and pick up on what others are feeling, getting to know the entire color wheel will be rather helpful. The more aware you are of the mixing of emotions and what effects can end up happening, the easier it will be to try and get what you want beforehand. Think back to the colors.

If an artist has no idea that blue and red make purple, they are just going to keep blending colors until they get something. What will end up happening is that they just mix every color together and get some sort of brown color! A talented artist will know how to blend and correct colors. A person with a high level of emotional intelligence will be aware of how emotions can be affected by things so minuscule.

Some emotions will be because of the same stimuli but based on an emotional reaction. For example, you might have a video released of you singing. You could either be proud or ashamed.

One feels good and one feels bad. If you are of a certain ethnicity, maybe you get offended by racist jokes while another person likes to make them. These are all based on our emotional connection to that stimuli. If your friend makes a rude comment to you, you might brush it off. If a stranger on the street shouted the same thing from their car, you'd want to run up and attack them!

A combination of the love for your friend and the understanding of the joke helped to alleviate the situation. For the person shouting from their car, the shock of that statement along with the hurt from the comment caused you to emotionally react and want to chase them down.

These combined emotions are assessed on their level of intensity felt by the individual as well. Maybe you and your friend are watching your favorite team play baseball. Your team loses brutally and you are both mad. You sit in silence for a bit, but you decide to shrug it off and open another beer. Your friend, on the other hand, gets up and throws their beer across the room, stepping outside to chain smoke while they calm down. You were both angry, but your friend felt that anger more intensely – potentially based on their past or simply based on their emotional intelligence - and reacted to it in a much stronger way.

While there is a basic underlying emotion to all that we feel, these kinds of more complex combined emotions will help us better articulate the things that we're actually feeling. When you can break apart these complex emotions, it becomes easier to also ensure that you can analyze the reaction typically associated (Donaldson, 2019).

### *Easy Emotions*

Easy emotions are ways to refer to those that come easier to us. These are feelings of happiness, love, joy, excitement, and positive surprise. Easy emotions are the ones that you feel when you are doing your favorite activity.

When you can get cozy on the couch and turn on your favorite show, belly full of some delicious takeout and not a care in the world, you do not have to think twice about how you feel. You might be ultra-appreciative and think, "how lucky am I?". But often, if this is a nightly routine as well, you will simply feel that emotion without having to put any effort into it.

When it comes to surprise, you might feel speechless, astonished, stimulated, amazed. Perhaps a friend surprised you with a birthday party and you are filled with joy. Not only is this a good feeling because you feel loved, but it is pleasing because it came naturally. You didn't have to think about getting surprised.

For joy, you might be feeling optimistic and hopeful. Perhaps a feeling of euphoria comes over you. Maybe you are satisfied, grateful, or proud. Maybe you just finished your semester with a report card that shows straight A's.

Finding out about a promotion could also be great news. It took a lot of negative emotions to get there but in that time when you are ultra-appreciative, you aren't thinking twice. You are usually basking in that easy emotion.

When it comes to love, you are feeling compassion, desire, and affection. Love can be incredibly complicated, do not get me wrong. It can make you feel all twisted up inside. But the good parts come easy. When you can just sit and chat with someone you really love, sharing jokes and having a good time, that's easy.

Love certainly is not romantic either; it is not just about feeling good during intimate moments. Love is when you have children and see their happy faces at the things you have provided. Love is holding your warm cat as you both snuggle up in bed at night. Love is seeing your mom after not visiting home for over a month. These things just happen. You might work hard to get them, but as you are feeling that emotion, it is simply something that you ride out.

Love is peaceful, it is romantic and sentimental. All of these words are ways to describe the combined emotions of the things that are good.

## Challenging Emotions

Challenging emotions are the ones that put us in bad moods. We do not want to refer to them as negative emotions because then that means that they are bad. We do not want to look at these as bad things because they come just as naturally to you like the easy ones. However, they are more challenging as we have them.

They are the emotions that we have to push through, confront, and sit in misery with as we deal with them. These challenging emotions are the ones that leave us thinking, "why me?" or ones that make us wish we were anywhere else. Challenging emotions can cause thoughts that we have to confront.

We might ask ourselves, "why am I thinking this way?". The challenging emotions are ones like regret, making us question if we are bad people. We might wonder if we have made too many mistakes, should we have done something different, or if there is any hope for us at all.

Sometimes, these challenging emotions are so hard to deal with that we will push them out of our heads. We can block out things we do not want to think about, thoughts we do not want to believe, all because they are just too hard to deal with.

If you are fearful, you might be insecure, dreading something, or in a panic. Perhaps every terrible scenario is playing out in your head before you have to attend an event. Maybe you are thinking about how the plane might crash before your vacation, or you might lose your luggage as you make it to the airport.

On a date, you might be thinking of all the terrible things that you are saying, wondering if you are making a fool of yourself. These emotions can pop into your head and some people are good at pushing them out. Others will latch onto these emotions like they are the truth, allowing them to control the direction of their actions.

Anger can build into rage, jealousy, and resentment. Perhaps a friend is living a life filled with everything you ever wanted and this makes you incredibly angry. That jealousy can soon turn into resentment toward that friend when that emotion is not dealt with.

Sometimes we will not even be aware of this kind of jealousy we feel. We might simply hate a person, only to realize later, once we're separated from that situation, that all along we were just jealous of someone that we hated so much.

You might be annoyed, frustrated, and agitated. Perhaps someone is just really getting on your nerves and driving you nuts. These aren't easy feelings to deal with. We question why they have to be the way they are or maybe question why we are so easily agitated.

Perhaps you are mortified, hostile, and exasperated. These are all just different words to describe a wide range of complex emotions that form as a result of varying combinations of basic feelings.

Then there are the sad feelings. You might be in agony, feeling hurt, and suffering. Perhaps you feel neglected or carry shame and sorrow. Maybe you are regretful, guilty, and remorseful. All of these kinds of thoughts can turn into rather intense feelings that stew and fester in our lives.

They can lead to intrusive thoughts that never seem to go away. We can obsess over the past, replaying things in our head over and over. Though it might seem like we will find an answer in the embarrassing memories we relive, they only cause us more agony.

Perhaps you are holding onto isolated feelings, you have no power, or are overwhelmed with grief. Simply feeling lonely can be a horrible feeling. Everything that we discussed in this section is not easy to deal with. Some people will internalize these feelings, hating themselves and becoming depressed or closed off.

Others might use these emotions to lash out at others, usually pushing people away. The best way to ensure these challenging emotions do not destroy our lives is to learn why we have them in the first place and how we can use them to actually enhance our lives.

## Why We Have Emotions

There is a biological purpose as to why we have emotions. Think about every purpose your body's functions serve. Your heart pumps blood everywhere to keep all your limbs alive. Your stomach processes what you eat, doing its best to get as many vitamins and nutrients as possible from each food source. Then your brain tells you what's right and what's wrong in the hopes that you'll make the best decision. What about our emotions, however? What purpose do these serve?

They are responses to different threats that we might be presented with. When you are angry at your spouse for keeping secrets from you, you feel threatened that something bad might happen. You are fearful over the end of your relationship and up until that point, part of your survival was dependent on your relationship.

The biological purpose of emotions has been to keep us alive. You are afraid of certain things and this can protect you. You are afraid of falling off a cliff so you might stay a little further back from the edge, your brain knowing the threat that this can have. When we're afraid of the dark, that can be something that dates back to more primal times when a predator might have been lurking in the dark bushes.

Emotions weren't only created so that we're scared all the time. They also came about through years of evolution because we need to be able to identify different opportunities. When a bowl of food looks especially tasty, we eat it because who knows if that will be the last time that we get to eat for a while. When we are given the chance to meet somebody new, we might feel positive emotions from this, knowing that they could end up being someone that changes our lives.

Emotions used to help us survive. When there was a threat, your body would go into either a "fight" or "flight" mode. You would sense that there was danger and thereafter, your body would ready itself for the best possible resolution to this attack. Think of it like an animal. If you ran up to your cat and started screaming and swatting at it, he is going to either scratch you back or sprint and hide under the bed. If you saw a bear in the wild and you were acting all loud and crazy, that bear might run and hide as well or they might completely destroy you (Stosny, 2019).

The fight mode gets your muscles tensed so that you know how to fight back. Your arms clench, your heart starts beating faster, and you ready yourself to start swinging fists should you have to. Your eyes widen and your attention focuses. This sort of adrenaline rush can make you feel somewhat "pumped up." Your body's trying to get ready to fight, so you have this sudden burst of energy. For some people, this can result in the idea that they need to push the fight further and get it going. In one way, it is them validating their own response, maybe trying to look for reasons that this fight is the best. Others might also do this as a way to have the upper hand.

Think of an especially inebriated buff college frat boy at a bar who wants to start a fight with someone that's pretty much a carbon copy of him. He might say something like, "come on bro, do you want to hit me?" egging him on and trying to get him to start the fight first. These are all just survival tactics when you really start to break things down.

The flight mode gets you ready to sprint as fast as you can. You might start to feel more anxious, as if you have to leave. Perhaps you have trouble breathing, feeling as though you need to get up and out of the room. You might shake your leg, feel your heartbeat, and look for the quickest exit. These kinds of responses, both the fight and flight, do not just happen physically.

Nowadays, we do not need to worry about a bear gobbling us up as we sit and relax, but we do need to be cautious of other factors for survival. You might be someone that never punched anyone in your life and never will. When you are presented with a threat, you might still respond in fight mode, however.

Let's say a friend starts to question your honesty, maybe calling you out on a lie they think you made. You might get defensive, feeling as though they are questioning your credibility. Rather than hearing them out to really get to the bottom of all the rumors, you could start questioning their credibility, taking their character in defense.

We can "flee" mentally as well. When someone is yelling or screaming at you, you might be the type of person to just shut down and start to disassociate from the situation. This happens often in abused children. They do not have the option to fight back because they aren't strong enough, but they can't flee because their parents are the only caregivers they know. It can be easy to just shut down and try to tune out what is going on as our body's way of fleeing the scene of the attack.

When you feel such negative emotions, it can be challenging to be able to look inwards about what the root issue is and why you might be feeling a certain emotion so intensely. Now that you understand the evolutionary purpose of these emotions, let's look at why you are still having them today and how you might be able to interpret them in a way that benefits your life.

## Motivation

Our motivation might sometimes also be referred to as our arousal. When something elicits a feeling of curiosity or gets us excited, that can lead to more feelings of exploration. One motivation for our emotional reactions is to simply explore them deeper and see what the root of them could be. We might like to test our limits, see what thrills us, and understand why we get so mad at some of the things that we do.

As the mammals that we are, we are wired to explore as a way to get the supplies we need. If you let a cat outside, they are going to start sniffing around, maybe eating bugs or looking for rats along the way. This curiosity is natural and part of their survival. This can be a reason that we might start to feel emotional connections to certain stimuli. Some things might give us interest, so we are motivated to discover even more.

Our motivation is a reaction to an emotion that therein helps us respond to the feelings that we might be having. All emotions can motivate us, even the more challenging ones. As we start to get more into discussing your control over your emotional intelligence now, start to think about how each feeling you have can be one that drives you.

Not every emotion will be a motivator. Some days you just might be in a bad mood and need to sleep and eat and relax. Other days, you might find that you are perfectly comfortable with just sitting with your happiness, basking in the glory of ignorant bliss.

### Interpretation

Of course, we can't only talk about our own emotions when referring to different human thoughts and feelings. We have to be aware of how others play into our emotional roles. Whether they are influencing how we feel or we are playing a role of persuasion in their lives, it is important to see how human emotions can all mingle together.

The major part of emotional intelligence is understanding how others are feeling. When we start to come to terms with the emotions that others have and really recognize what it is they might be feeling, that is when real persuasion can start to happen.

We need to recognize how perception can entirely change someone's ability to emotionally react.

How you perceive someone's emotion can be different from others as well. Maybe you leave a party and say, "didn't she seem mad?" and someone else says, "what are you talking about?". You can pick up on, and equally misunderstand, something that another person has the opposite perspective on.

Others might perceive your emotion completely different from what you are trying to express as well. Maybe you are really in a good mood, but just feeling exhausted. Others might see a lack of excitement as a sign you are in a bad mood, constantly asking you "what's wrong?".

To see emotions in others requires you to have a strong understanding of what they look like in yourself first.

As you start to become an emotional master, both of your own and other's feelings, it becomes so much easier to understand emotional awareness. When we fully improve our perception of emotion, we will start to better use it to drive logic and influence decision making.

# Emotion versus Logic and Decision Making

Many decisions are based on emotions over logic and we aren't always aware of this connection. Now we are really going to start to get into why all this matters to you as an entrepreneur. Of course, we first had to go into detail over what emotions were and what it can mean to feel certain things. Throughout the rest of the book, we are going to put an emphasis on why it is crucial you maintain a high level of emotional intelligence.

We might start to get fearful, so we rush something that we know should take time and patience. We might get angry, so we cut connections that would be better off improved. If we use emotions, we react too quickly, not giving ourselves any time to see what would be the most beneficial in the situation overall.

We also need to ensure that we are able to use emotion in our sales in order to drive decision-making in the people that we want to influence. Emotions can be very strong and they can be what helps us to finally win over clients and convince investors that we are worth their money.

You'll first need to start to be fully aware of the emotions that have been driving your decisions. How has happiness, fear, anger, and sadness played into your decision-making process?

Emotions shouldn't be totally removed from our ability to choose whether something is good or bad, but it shouldn't take the front wheel and drive that decision overall.

Let's start to look at the models of emotional intelligence so we can better pick up the ability to figure out how to improve our own (Levine, 2019).

# Chapter 2 – The EQ Models

In this chapter, we are going to discuss the different emotional intelligence models. You know you better than anyone else, or you should at least. Though talking to other people can really help you get to know yourself more. For the most part, you have a true sense of self around your identity that's stronger than what other people think.

When it comes to understanding your emotional intelligence, it can be hard to measure. What's important is understanding the difference between what you think you would do in any given situation and what you would actually do.

Now that we know everything there is to know about emotions (if only...), we can move onto what emotional intelligence is. Emotional intelligence is similar to your intelligence quotient

Your emotional intelligence is the ability for you to manage your own emotions, while also recognizing and understanding the emotional state of those around you.

Emotional intelligence is objective. You are able to see the good qualities that you have to offer the world, while also being conscious of the things it wouldn't hurt to work on. Simply being self-aware does not always equate to self-loathing. There is such a thing as being too aware. This might get to the point where you become scared or paranoid, maybe thinking everyone hates you, always ruminating over the things you said. Most people aren't even going to be aware of these smaller things about yourself that you might pick up on.

Someone emotionally intelligent understands there is important influence that you need to be aware of on one level, while still being able to see that you are a beneficial and influential person in other ways.

Someone emotionally intelligent understands that they are in charge of their emotional reactions – not necessarily their emotions. You might not be able to help it if you get mad that your sport's team lost, but you are 100% in charge of whether or not you choose to punch a wall.

If your emotional intelligence is high, then that means you have a high ability of influence by using your emotions. This means that you can understand how critical thinking can affect your exact emotions.

One quick method to improve intelligence is The Six Seconds model. You should notice three things, all in just a couple seconds. Know yourself and what you do, choose to do what you need to do, and decide to do this for a reason. It can be vague but, essentially, it is a great way to determine where you are at in your emotional intelligence ability. When someone makes you mad, you might know that they offended you, choose to insult them and do this because you want to make yourself feel better. That would demonstrate a low level of emotional intelligence.

Each of these models gives us insight into what emotional intelligence is and what level you might "score" at in each of these categories.

# Ability

This model was developed by two different people, Perter Salovey of Yale University, as well as John Mayer, who attended the University of New Hampshire.

This first model is a newer version of a way to define what a person's emotional intelligence level is. You can decide where you might be based on coming up with your own scores.

Is what we're describing behavior that sounds like you or do you think you could honestly work on it a bit? When thinking of these kinds of scenarios, ask yourself if you think that other people would answer for you. It can be helpful to consider another's view on you in an objective way.

Many of us can be emotionally intelligent without even trying. It's not always something that you have to practice and can just be a part of who you are. However, the ability model helps to point out areas of weaknesses that you might want to work on (Salovey, Brackett & Mayer, 2007).

### *Ability to Perceive Emotions*

The first part of the model is inclusive of how nonverbal signals are understood and processed by an individual. Those with social disabilities, such as social anxiety or Asperger's, might struggle with picking up on what others are trying to say not through their verbal language.

If someone is in a rush, we might see them tapping their foot, anxiously wanting to leave. If someone is sad, they might not be making eye contact, frowning, and unfocused. There are plenty of little cues that let us know how the other person might be feeling without them having to say anything.

Any facial expression or body movement; whether it is in a picture, in their voice, through their words, or whatever else, can be an indication of a person's emotion. Can you pick up on the things about a person that might signal what emotion they are feeling? Can you tell when someone might be feeling uncomfortable? Do you understand what it means when someone is wanting to leave?

This doesn't just go for how you recognize emotions in others either, it is also important to note how you might be able to recognize different emotions in yourself. Let's say that you are in one of those moods where everything annoys you. Maybe your assistant asks a question and you get a little snappy, a friend texts you about dinner and you are quick to write it off. Even the cat might get on your nerves to the point you feel like exploding.

Are you able to recognize that it is not all of these people that are annoying, that instead, you are just in a grumpy mood? Though the initial emotion might be annoyance, how well can you say to yourself, "OK, I just need to destress a bit before I snap on anyone else.". It can be easy to blame everyone else for our bad mood, but those with a skilled ability to understand all emotional perception will have a higher EQ.

### Emotional Reasoning

How well can one use emotions to cognitively investigate? How well can emotional activity spark intellectual exploration? Do you notice one of your behaviors and have the ability to link it back to something in the past? Are you able to take a terrible mood and turn it into a moment where you learn something deep about yourself?

When you have a desired outcome, there is a way that you can use both your emotion and the emotion of another person in order to guide you both in the direction of the things that you want. Are you able to catch someone in a good mood and use that in order to inspire them? Perhaps you and someone else are both in a distant or even lazy-feeling mood and you take that opportunity to just have a chill day.

Are you considerate of others' emotions while making decisions? Most of the time we do what is best for us while making sure no one else gets hurt. Do you allow yourself to make some sacrifices so that you can get to a decision that's best for the both of you?

Are you appropriate with the expression and discussion of emotions? Can you bring up things that make you upset in the right setting? It's never easy to talk about our feelings, but someone with a higher EQ knows that it is vital to have moments of discussion and reflection in personal relationships.

## *Understanding Emotions*

Can you recognize the emotion that someone is displaying? It can be easy to think that someone is mad but sometimes that is just our insecurities getting the best of us. We might think everyone hates us or is judging us, when we're really fine and just feeling extra sensitive to scrutiny.

Once you recognize these emotions, how well are you able to interpret them to find the most realistic situation? Is someone mad because no one came to their party or is someone mad because they are really feeling lonely and angry at their friends? Can you push past the surface level idea and really see the root of why someone is upset?

Do you get why people are mad, even in situations that wouldn't make you angry? It's easy to write someone off and say, "I do not get why they are mad," but understanding why someone is mad doesn't mean that you have to agree with the reaction. You can still see their hurt without feeling the offense yourself.

Are you understanding of the complexity that one emotion could hold? Once you start to see how deep feelings can really go, it becomes easier to start to understand why someone might be displaying that certain thought or feeling.

Do you have the ability to look past just the words someone is saying and really get what feelings they want to express?

## *Management of Emotions*

Are you able to regulate your own emotions? When you stub your toe, this is a good sign of how well you have your emotions under control. Can you walk it off and feel fine or do you have to scream a loud curse word? When someone cuts you off in traffic, can you wave and smile or do you feel the need to lay on your horn and tail them? No one is wrong for having the initial upset feeling, but there are many different ways that emotion can be taken, and it is not always good.

How well can you articulate a response and keep it appropriate to the situation? Even though you might have the urge to say something rude, are you able to just keep your cool and shrug the comment off or do you have to say something equally snarky right back?

Do you have trouble responding immediately to an emotion you have? Do you make impulsive decisions? Maybe the server came up and said your food is going to be out ten minutes later than they said. Can you simply say, "ok, that's fine, thanks!" or do you throw a fit that gets the attention of the entire restaurant?

Do you often apologize for your behavior after it has happened? There are many people that will snap, yell, fight, and argue but ten minutes later apologize. Even though it is good to recognize it and say you are sorry, it is not good to consistently snap like this, simply hoping every time that others will just so easily forgive.

Does stress cause it to be more challenging to focus? Do you have trouble liking someone when they have upset you? How well do other people's emotions affect you as well? All four of these sections are ways that you can start to measure your emotional intelligence. They represent different branches of emotions and how they are utilized. In order to be emotionally intelligent, you have to have all four working in harmony, not some that are great and others that aren't. The more you work on these, the better and stronger they will all become individually as well.

# Mixed

This model is one that we will likely be referring to the most because it is so detailed yet inclusive of the basic ideas understood in the other sections. It was created by Daniel Goleman, whom we referred to in the introduction (Goleman, 1995).

## *Self-Awareness*

This is inclusive of one's confidence. Do you have the ability to recognize that you are a valuable person who matters in the world? We can easily see how we affect the world, but it is important to be conscious of all the ways you have been able to positively affect those around you.

Do you recognize the strengths that you have? These will be the things that you do well, what others admire in you, the things others ask you to do often, and simply, the things that you love to do the most. Even if you are not necessarily a good singer but still love singing, this is still a trait that many will admire!

Can you identify what weaknesses you might run into? Do you need to work on communicating? Maybe you have to increase your level of self-discipline? Whatever it might be, someone with high EQ levels understands what they need to focus on strengthening.

They will also have the ability to recognize their own feelings. Can you tell what makes you upset, identify your triggers, and work through your inner turmoil on your own? Those with a low EQ will not be self-aware. They will not understand why they are in a bad mood; they might treat others with disregard and they will often be self-loathing and overly judgmental.

### Self-Regulation

Do you have the ability to display self-control? When we're kids, teens, and even young adults it is easy to look at the authority figures to tell us what to do. You have to wake up and go to school, do your homework by a certain deadline, and do your best to follow the rules the rest of the time. Now that we're adults, we're the ones in charge! Are you able to come up with your own schedule and actually stick to the things you say you are going to do?

Are you trustworthy? Do you struggle to keep secrets, or find yourself enjoying the discussions of others? We all like our occasional gossip or the juicy news on the street, but consistently discussing another person and breaking them down when they are not even there is not healthy. You might like to share the secret that your co-worker's spouse got arrested for public indecency, but if you and your mom constantly talk about your sister and all the problems she has and never discuss this with her in person, this can show a low level of emotional intelligence.

How well can you adapt to any given situation? Do you have the ability to take control over yourself and cool down when you have to suddenly switch plans? When things didn't go your way, are you able to make sure that this doesn't cause you discomfort, or to grow really angry?

## *Motivation*

Motivation is one's ability to use their emotions for a beneficial drive. Can these feelings you have become something that actually powers you into a beneficial action? Maybe you are feeling angry. You could drink a beer, and then another, and then another, and then another until you are so numb you do not feel any pain. Or, you could go on a run and release your anger, come home and enjoy a reasonable amount of beer while you joke and hang out with close friends. It's not like you aren't allowed to have fun, in terms of enjoying alcohol, but it is about how your motivation to do certain things might be driven by positive or negative emotions.

Not only are you motivated, but are you committed? We all have great ideas all the time, but how many of those ideas turn into half-planned ventures? By being an entrepreneur, you are already doing a great job of turning your goal into actionable steps; what's important going forward is the level of dedication you have to this.

Do you take initiative when you know that it is needed? Sometimes we know what's best to do, but we might be too afraid to start. When you know what needs to be done and you have the ability to take the lead, then this will be a good sign of your emotional intelligence.

How optimistic are you about what it is that seems motivational? Optimism can sometimes be blinding and we always need to pay special attention to the things that could go wrong. However, if we're motivated, then we're optimistic and we need to ensure we have the right balance of both.

## Empathy

Empathy is your ability to not just understand, but to feel the emotions of those around you. We will get into this a little later in the book, but for now, empathy refers to one's ability to feel what it is that others might be also feeling. Can you relate to that pain? Can you understand what it feels like to go through what it is that they are experiencing?

This is important to have because you need to also be politically aware of the world, at least your society, and the diversity required in your team.

## Social Skills

Finally, social skills, leadership, communication abilities, and conflict resolution are incredibly important in measuring your emotional intelligence in this model. Again, we're going to dive deeper into the important social skills that are needed, especially as an entrepreneur. Be conscious of how you are able to interact within this world, as it can show what your level of emotional intelligence might be.

How can you take all four of these things we just discussed and apply them in a way that helps others?

# Trait

Konstantin Vasily Petrides defined this model by referring to it as a constellation. He believed that our emotional self-created perceptions are based on emotion and these would become the drivers of our personality (Srivastava, 2013).

Now that you have a better idea of what your emotional intelligence level might be, let's take a look at how this can directly affect your personality.

It's important to remember that just because you have a high level of emotional intelligence doesn't mean that everyone else will always see that. Since you perceive others in ways differently than someone else might, others will perceive you different as well. While you might be an emotionally intelligent person with a really high score, that doesn't mean that others will always see you as empathetic because they have their own personal perceptions.

In the next chapter, we will start to breakdown more about how you are going to be able to influence others based on improving the skills and emotions we talked about throughout this chapter.

This model forms more around the idea that your EQ is based on personality traits, not necessarily your ability. So rather than asking, how well can you do this, it is whether or not you can do that if it is part of your personality.

The trait model is one based in your own self-perception of how you can emotionally manage. Some reject this model on the basis of self-assessment.

How well can you understand your own emotions? Do you also have the ability to be aware of how others might be perceiving some of your emotions?

With this trait model, you have to really look at your personality in the past and your history of choices you have made, rather than the "what-ifs" of what you might do now.

One has to have an understanding of their personality framework in order to better recognize their ability to judge their emotional intelligence level in the first place.

# Chapter 3 – Introspection

In this chapter, we are going to focus more on the EQ levels as much as possible. By this point, you should already understand of someone with both a high and a lower EQ level might look like. We went over the levels of a high emotionally intelligent person in the last chapter – someone that can recognize emotions in themselves and others and use those for good. Those who have lower emotional intelligence will be reactionary and dismissive of the feelings and thoughts of people around them.

This chapter, we are going to be discussing the way that you can recognize emotions within yourself. This is going to be directed in a business and sales way now as well. Rather than talking about personal relationships you have with friends and family; we are going to keep your attention on what matters the most as an entrepreneur. You can still apply these kinds of ideas to your personal life but in the context that we're discussing, it is all about making business relationships and focusing on sales regulation.

The point of all of this will be to help you understand the importance of sales negotiation. That is why you are applying this to your own business, after all. You want to learn how to be an emotionally intelligent person to ensure that you are focused on business when it matters – never your emotional feelings that could derail a sale. That sounds cold and calculated, so it is also vital to remember how our emotions can still play an imperative role in our lives. You shouldn't react emotionally right away, but you should still let your feelings and passion help to drive success overall. The key is using your emotions for something beneficial, not in a way that could make things worse.

There will also be an emphasis on relationship management. Where does relationship management start? With yourself, of course. The next chapter will be more focused on emotional intelligence with others but right now, we are going to emphasize building your emotional intelligence within yourself first.

## Self-Awareness and Self-Esteem

You are likely already more self-aware now than you were at the beginning of the reading. What you need to work on now is how you can be more self-aware in your business. You are the boss; you are in charge. You're the manager of managers, the head guy, the number one that everyone will go to at the end of the day. There are already expectations of you in place before you even get a chance to meet some of your employees and clients. It is up to you to now focus on getting into the right mindset to operate as an emotionally intelligent individual.

Always look for ways that you can give to others first. Be aware of how you wouldn't be successful if it weren't for the people that are working just as hard under you. Give without expecting anything in return. Give and forget that you did, so that you will not be waiting around for others to give back to you. Don't give to a point where you are sacrificing yourself and do not give often to someone that you do not think would do the same for you if they could. Not everyone is going to give back to you but remember, when you might feel guilty about not giving enough, would they do the same for you?

While being self-aware, always look for ways that you can improve. What do you feel you need to do to help your team? How can you also help them in return? You might try to figure this out through surveying your team. Be cautious; however, as not everyone is always going to be too open to chit chatting with the boss about what their problem is. Look for ways that you can give people a voice without them being afraid to share. Do surveys, and anonymous ones will help people be open even more.

While being critical is an important aspect of being self-aware, you must also ensure that you are doing your best to have a high level of self-esteem. You have to believe in yourself first if you ever expect anyone else to believe in you as well. Having high self-esteem doesn't mean thinking that you are better than everyone else. It means that you know your own worth and it doesn't always matter if everyone else feels the same way.

Always put yourself in your employee's position. Yes, you need to focus on yourself, but how can you really improve your business if you do not know what it is like to be the middleman? Don't expect things from your employees if you wouldn't be able to do the same, at least in their situation. If you are the owner of a construction business but do not know how to operate a certain piece of machinery, that's understandable. However, if you had their same training, would you feel comfortable doing what you are asking of your employees?

Be aware of how much work you are putting in as well. Depending on the position, you should be working just as often as your employees. A great manager will also do the same things that they are asking of their employees. They do not want to feel as though they are working forty + hours a

51

week when you are only available for one hour a week. You can't do it all, especially the larger your business is, but you can still make an effort to show to others that you are willing to work just as hard as them.

## Confidence and Assertiveness

Part of being self-aware is also going to involve having confidence. There's a difference in being assured and being someone that is too cocky. Don't be afraid to say what's on your mind, but phrase it in a way that others will respond well to. Let's say you run a small clothing store. You walk in one day and notice that one of your employees is leaning up against the counter on their phone and there are a few out-of-place clothing items on a messy rack.

Your first instinct is going to be, "doesn't anyone do any work around here?"; however, this will just instill fear in the employee. Instead, you might still be wondering what the reason for the messy store is, but you'll want to phrase it in a way that can turn into a productive conversation.

That will give you a little insight into what was going on and give you the chance to express concerns over their work ethic. You might say something like, "it looks like it was a busy day, were you able to get a lot done?" They might proceed to tell you the tasks they did and you could ask something afterward like, "have you been able to get to the clothing racks yet? I noticed one is a little messed up over there." This helps the employee give an explanation.

They might say something about how they just got a chance to catch their breath after a rush or that they needed to take a quick break in between cleaning up. This is understandable and you could remind them of your appreciation for their work. This employee could have been lying to you, but they will still be more likely to respect you and want to improve their own work because they respect your authority.

They might also say something about how they didn't notice and reveal that it wasn't that busy of a day at all. You'll then be able to use this moment to tell them that when the store is slow, they need to pay more attention to keeping the racks tidy. This is going to be based in your own words but as you can see, their revealing of the lack of work that day shows they aren't doing the tasks they are supposed to be performing. It gives you a chance to educate them so that they do better next time, while still in a respectful and authoritative way.

Confidence means that you believe in yourself. You accept that you are not perfect, but you know that you have the ability to do what needs to be done with the supplies already at your disposal. Too much confidence can make you seem frightening and that will not give your employees any respect over you. When you are around, they'll do their best. But when they have free reign, they'll probably slack off because they will not really care about the business. They might believe that you do not respect them, so they will not show that back to you.

The same goes for when you are working with clients and contractors. You'll want to show them that you are open to discussion and approachable. You will not be able to give them everything they want, even if they are especially demanding. Confidence doesn't mean rudely telling them no. you simply have to find a way that the both of you can benefit and communicate the reality in an effectively authoritative manner. We'll get more into working with others in the next chapter.

Part of lacking confidence is having the difficulty to say "no." This is a vital word that we need to include in our vocabulary, if we ever plan on getting the things that we want. Sometimes, we can get afraid to tell people "no," because we grow fearful that they will not need us anymore. If anyone is only around you because they need you and like how frequently you say "yes," then they are not someone that you should focus your energy on.

This is where we fall into being assertive. An emotionally intelligent person is aware of what they want and knows how to get it. They aren't blinded by power, but they are able to see a situation that will benefit them while also aiding others in the process. When you are only focused on your goals, you lose sight of what is right, what is fair.

When you are only focused on everyone else, then you forget about yourself and you can quickly become exhausted, losing some of your identity on the way. Focus on finding the balance between pleasing others while ensuring you are still taking care of yourself.

At the same time, you also want to assess when their wants are things that aren't going to harm anyone else. For example, you are going to want to pick and choose some battles. Accept that not everything that you want is going to be realistic. Ensure that you aren't hurting anyone else along the way.

When you are confident, more people will believe in you. When you aren't afraid to stand up for what you want, it shows that you are trustworthy as well.

Remember that there is a huge difference between just being a boss and being someone that manages others. Don't just tell people what to do; work with them to make sure they understand what they need to do. Don't just say "yes" to everyone that makes requests through your business. Explain to them the process and give them flexibility, maybe a few options to choose what they feel most comfortable with. When you open these doors of communication, then it can help you build relationships. Don't think of yourself as just a business owner. You are a facilitator between people that want your service or product and others that want to help you in return for something valuable as well, whether it is money from income or simply experience through internships. It's not just a business transaction, even if that's what your business boils down to. There is a valuable exchange between all parties and your confidence and assurance are required to see this.

You want to be assertive, but never aggressive. You might be able to gain power with anger and being more aggressive, but you will never gain respect. Your employees having respect for you is going to be more important than anything else.

### *How to Make Requests as a Socially Intelligent Person*

A socially intelligent person knows how to make requests. It can be scary to ask for things at times but once you learn how to do it, it can come so easily. First, remember that you are entitled to ask for things from others. There are some entrepreneurs that will even be afraid to ask their own employees for help! That's what others are there for! As long as you communicate in an effective way and be open and honest with others, you are never wrong for making a request.

Those with a high EQ level ensure that what they are asking of others is first and foremost, reasonable. Never ask someone of something you wouldn't be willing to do for them, again, if they were in the same position. Let's say you need a personal loan from a friend for around $10,000 and since they net over $1,000,000 a year in their business, it is really not that much money.

As a struggling entrepreneur, it is a lot for you. Of course, if they asked you for that money, you would have to say no because you do not have it. However, if you were in his position, would you be able to say "yes," to what it is that you are requesting? If you say "no," then it is probably something you shouldn't ask.

When making requests, keep it as simple as possible. The more reasons that you give for someone to listen to you and help you out, the more ideas you are giving them for reasons not to help you out.

If you need that loan and you start to say, "well I need it because it is just money to get me started, and I ran out of my funds already, and I need to buy a bunch of things, but I'll get it back to you soon," and ramble on with more and more excuses, then you are basically listing out all the reasons the other person would say "no."

They'll see that you need money to get started, which means there's a chance that you will not finish. Then they'll hear that you ran out of funds, which means that you might not be good with money, and so on. Each of these reasons why you need the money can be twisted into a reason that they should not give you the money.

When making requests, frame it in a way that will benefit them, and never lie. This doesn't mean you have to give the juicy details. Simply state your request, tell them you understand if they must decline and from there, you can communicate. They might ask "why" anyway, but this gives you time to prepare a proper response that will not scare them away from the request.

Ask yourself if you would feel comfortable with the request. If you think it is absurd, then you probably are asking a little too much. Never bank your requests on luck.

Find a way that the other person's needs will be met by your request. Start by telling them how you'll be helping them before you even get into how you'll be helped.

Never lie. Sometimes you might want to exaggerate one part to make another look less atrocious. However, lying is one way to instantly make everyone else around you untrustworthy of your actions.

Never show emotion when you do not get what you want. Maybe a client says "no," or someone else refuses to invest. It might be a denial that really changes the course of how you thought things were going to go. Perhaps you were really banking on their saying, "yes," so you get emotional and upset. Don't show this with anger. It's OK to be disappointed, but you do not want to take it out on them for turning you down.

Don't burn bridges. Some people say that it is fine to burn bridges because then that means you will not be tempted to look back. Sure, there's a reason that you left in the first place. However, if you continue to burn bridges, you might find that you eventually become isolated on your own island!

Don't put pressure on anyone, even if it is a really pressing matter. They might say yes, but you do not want to be in a position where they later withdrawal, realizing that your request was too much for them. Let's say that you asked your business partner for a loan and once they approved, that gave you the chance to make another small investment for your business based on a lead from a different colleague.

However, when you asked your partner, you really put the pressure on them. They said no at first and it took a lot of convincing to get them to cave. While you might have won, he might end up pulling out. Then you have already invested the money, putting you in an even more challenging position than if you would have just dealt with him saying "no" in the first place.

## Asking Others for Help

When it comes to asking for help, always do so in a way that you will be able to pay the other person back. This is not for the exact monetary amount but look for a way that you can help them too. Never just ask for help and then abandon the other person. This will only make things worse for you down the line.

Let those who are helping to guide you as well. Don't just ask for one aspect. Don't pretend like you "know it all," when they are responding. If they start to offer you advice, take it. Maybe you ask for some help promoting your business through a friend. They agree, but they also make some suggestions to your branding that you do not totally agree with. Rather than turning them down right away, maybe you take part of their advice and twist in a way that works to your advantage.

They clearly know what they are doing or else you wouldn't be asking them for help. Listen to them and they will appreciate that you are willing to grow. They will then be more willing to help you out if you need it again in the future, rather than if you would have ignored them and blew off their suggestions.

Tell them the reason that you are asking for help in the first place. Maybe they'll be able to come up with a better solution for the issue at hand. If you ask for $1,000 in investments from someone but they do not feel comfortable giving you that money, perhaps you can throw in additional labor or a higher percentage of return if they do go through with the investment. They might counter with a better offer that saves both of you money, while you still get the outcome you were hoping for when making the initial request for the investment.

Let the other person know that you specifically chose them to help you out. Use phrases like:

"I asked you because I knew I could trust you."

"I do not feel comfortable asking anyone else."

Of course, only say these things if it is the truth, but it really is a good way to be more personable and show just how much you appreciate what they decided to do for you. These phrases make the other person feel important and they will be more willing to help because you have added compassion. Again, this is part of the process of building a relationship, not just working the motions of a transaction.

Remember that when you ask for help, you can never be too grateful. Send a "thank you" card, have them over for a nice steak dinner, buy them tickets to a fun show, or do whatever other small gesture you can. If they gave you a $100,000 loan, even taking them out to dinner once could be enough to show how much you really appreciate what they did for you.

Make sure that your timing is right. Don't wait until they are stressed. It can be tempting to ask when you know you will not have to face them. Maybe you leave a voicemail when you know they are not home, so you do not have to talk in person.

Don't do this! People will be so much more likely to respond when you take time out of your day to ask for help.

Don't bombard with gifts first. It will make people think that they are being bribed or that you only care to do nice things because you need something from them. It might seem like a good idea to take them out to dinner, get a little wine in them and ask when they are in good spirits. It could work, but it could also make them feel like they are being set up. Instead, ask them up front or at least preface the dinner by saying, "I want to take you out because I have something really important I need to ask." The more honest you are, the more likely they'll be willing to help out. Most people will say "yes" in times that they are able to fully help, so it will not always be a matter of whether or not they can do it; it can sometimes be up to whether or not they feel like they want to do it based on if they should be helping you out.

## Self-Regulation and Self-Control

It's important that we are aware of the impulsive behaviors we might exhibit in the workspace. If you are feeling anxious, maybe business is dying, your employees lack motivation, and clients are pulling out left and right, you might start to panic.

It can be easy to want to do something drastic; maybe fire someone, rearrange the office, change the logo, take out a loan for marketing, or do something else that you think will help you out of the rut.

Practice self-control and remember that most good things will take time. You will not just snap out of that rut. Have meetings, talk with employees, get candid with clients, and find ways to improve over time rather than demanding the situation gets fixed right away.

Part of having self-control is practicing patience. Just as mothers and fathers are models for their children, so are you for your employees!

When it comes to your personal life, you need to consistently regulate how this might transition into your work life. Are you always on vacation? Do you bring designer purses into work? Your employees will see this! Do not flaunt your wealth in front of them. They will start to resent you because they can't go on vacation as often or they have to wear used clothes because they will not have as much money for nicer designer pieces.

Regulate how much of that personal life you share with others as well. It can be tempting to talk to your employees because they will always be willing to listen, but they are not people to always spill all the drama to. Being personal is important, but there are some things that shouldn't be involved in a boss-employee relationship.

You must have self-control as well. Make sure that you are staying until the time that you were scheduled. If you are leaving every day an hour before time is up just because you can, then you are letting others know that you do not care about the business. If you do have to leave early, make sure you express why and keep your phone on you to check emails an hour after others are scheduled just to show that you are willing to still work.

Discipline yourself to stay on track with your goals as well. Don't be tempted to "sell out" for more money if it means that you are going against the original ideas of the business. There might be times when you have to make sacrifices for the company, but do not do it in a way that jeopardizes the future. Plan ahead and even though something might seem like a quick fix, ask if it is just a Band-Aid or the long-term solution to ensure you do not fall back into a place such as that again.

### Dealing with Stress Created by Yourself

A lot of the stress we feel comes from things that we have created within ourselves. When we do not control our anxious thoughts, they can turn into paranoid delusions rather quickly. We have to constantly check and see if the things that we are worried about are valid or if we are taking things way out of proportion.

You need to make sure that you are setting a time period away from work. You should have at least a quarter to a half a day every week that you go radio silent. Maybe it is Sunday from 8 am to 2 pm, or Friday nights after 6 you refuse to check your email. No matter how bad you might want to look, just give yourself some peace and quiet away from the job. Ideally, you'll dedicate a little more time, especially if your business is not even open every day. For a store that's open over 12 hours a day Monday-Sunday, it is hard to not always be there. Someone's always calling off or there's an especially angry customer. However, the business will survive for a few hours without you.

As entrepreneurs, it is hard to not constantly be stressed out. For many of our employees, they can simply clock out and go home! That's not so easy for us to do. Instead, we carry the weight of work with us wherever we go because it is our life! Don't let your business be the boss of you, however.

Allow other people to do some tasks. If you have to hire a temporary position or even a part-time one just to alleviate stress, do it! You might lose out on some income because you have to pay for the work, but it is better than paying the hospital bills after a stress-induced heart attack!

Don't let past failures trigger you into a panic. Treat each new venture as its own. Perhaps signs of decreasing business have started and ones similar to a last failed business adventure. Take this time to look at what you did wrong and how you can make this business different. Remember that not every dip in income means that the business is failing. Sometimes there will just be slow periods. Keep in mind that usually, when it rains, it pours.

Recognize when the stress first starts. Identify your triggers. Maybe it is the constant phone calls, the one client that always seems to need something, or an employee who is not living up to their part. Try and work through these stresses, find ways to avoid them, or come up with a solution to alleviate the stress that they bring on.

Always combat your stressful thoughts. When you have a negative one, come back at it with a positive one. An emotionally intelligent entrepreneur is going to know how to turn negative thoughts into ones that will provide them with use.

# Positive and Negative Emotions in Yourself

There are ways that you can manage the negative emotions.

You should never block out these kinds of negative emotions. The moment that you start to do this is when you start to build up and hold onto emotions that will only cause you more stress!

When it comes to your negative emotions, imagine that you are a mentor to someone else starting their own business. How would you help them to combat those ideas?

Let that negative emotion tell you something about both yourself and your business. What is it that you are afraid of losing?

How can you take that instance and, at the very least, learn from this negative emotion?

We make mistakes that turn into lessons. You might invest too much money at once and you learn that you need to start small once that investment fails. How can you take that negative feeling and learn from it before any mistakes are even made?

We will also want to put an emphasis on leveraging the positive emotions. Your mind is clearly one of greatness, that's how you have been able to become an entrepreneur. Every thought you have can be useful, it is simply up to you to find that overall purpose.

Always look for a change when everything else fails! Remember all that excitement at the beginning of your business adventure? How can you turn that around now and use it for something positive?

When you are angry, how can that passion be directed towards improving some aspect of your business?

Remember that you are always going to be anxious and fearful of the future. You just have to now focus on putting that energy to good use and using it as a passion-driver, not something that destroys you and your company.

# Self-Motivation

The key to motivation is knowing what needs to be done. What is it that you want to do? What is the goal of your business? You are not just an entrepreneur; you are a leader. You are someone established who is in charge of directing many people's lives.

If it is just to make money – be honest with yourself! We would all probably just sit around and relax, lay in the sun and eat if we could. But we have to make that money! Now that you have gotten that part out of the way, how else can this business add value? You might be able to make a ton of cash, but how can you make others' lives better? How can you make yourself feel more fulfilled?

Money is not the only thing that should drive you, either. You need to find a way that this method of making money is good for you and for others. An emotionally intelligent entrepreneur can take that passion and let it be the driver, the conductor, the pilot.

A successful entrepreneur knows exactly what needs to be done and they believe themselves. They see a goal and, even if it seems big, they have the confidence to know that they are the ones that can do it.

Motivation is necessary because no one else is going to tell you what to do. You have to start to take charge of your own life and the things that are the most important. Other people will be happy for you. Those that love you will encourage you. No one else but you is going to be able to take charge and really guide your life. You are the one that has to decide where things go from here.

You have to be confident and compassionate for yourself if you want to find true motivation. Though it can be hard to not be self-deprecating and critical, you will still want to stay focused on encouraging yourself, especially when going through times of others doubting you.

Motivation is going to be developed around goals. Come up with personal goals, goals for your team, goals for the next month, six months, year, five years, ten years, and so on.

Your goals need to be realistic. What goals would you give to an employee? If you wouldn't expect someone else to be able to achieve a certain goal within a timeframe, you can't always expect yourself to do it either.

Make sure to have a looming goal that you want to reach. What is it that you want to do with your life? You can't just want to be rich! You should want to do something great. Do you want to help people? Do you want to be remembered? Do you want to improve the earth?

What is it that you would be comfortable doing, knowing it was your greatest accomplishment before this great life ends? This should be your main goal and the one which helps to drive all the smaller goals along the way. Once you have determined what your biggest dream really is, it will be much easier to figure out the small steps you need to get there. If you wanted to move a mountain, you wouldn't do it by pushing the whole thing. You would want to start by moving one stone at a time.

# Chapter 4 – Extrospection

Extrospection is a way that you not only get to know other people, but you learn more about yourself in the process of learning from other people. If you stayed in your apartment all day every day, never leaving or interacting with others, eventually, you would start to become more anti-social, just by default. You might become more focused on yourself, only seeing the world through your perspective. When we get outside and consistently interact with others, it becomes a lot easier to start to learn more about ourselves and who we are.

As you continue to interact with others, you will start to see your ability to understand their needs better, also helping you figure out your own wants and desires. When you can really connect with someone and get to know who they are deep down, it starts to become easier to see what they are trying to say without only listening to their words.

As much as you might be able to control your own emotions and figure things out on your own, you will still always want to put an emphasis on ensuring that you are open and listening to others. Some people have a bad habit of sitting there and thinking about what they are going to say in response while another person is talking. They will not listen to anything the other has said and rather rehearse the conversation over and over again in order to make sure that they "win" the conversation. When you really listen to the other person and open yourself up to hear what they have to say, then you will start to explore some amazing things about both yourself and that other person.

# Recognizing Emotions in Others

Once you have recognized your own emotions within yourself, it is time to start recognizing them in other people. Part of really getting to know how someone else feels involves being empathetic to their needs. You'll need to understand their background and how that might have affected them as well. You will not get to know everything about your colleagues and employees when it comes to their personal life. It will still be helpful to try and have an idea of who they were before they became a part of your entrepreneurial adventure.

It is important that you learn to recognize emotions in other people for your own social well-being. You will get a better sense of when certain things are appropriate and when you should really just leave things as they are and not try to alter the situation. When someone is bad at reading social cues, it can show that they might have a lowered emotional intelligence.

When you can tell someone is mad, frustrated, or annoyed; you can accurately treat that situation. You might be able to help them calm down. Perhaps distracting them from that temporary emotion is all they will need to better focus on something else and work through their feelings.

When you can see that they are happy, you can encourage that behavior and aide them in growing stronger. You'll know what their happy mood is and assisting other people in being happy will really help your business. You will be able to see if they are feeling good and you will not have much work to do! If they are seemingly blue, you can brainstorm a plan to help them feel a little better.

You will be able to point out their weaknesses and the good things they do as well. This will make it easier to guide or praise. You can see what might trigger someone to not perform their best. Maybe you put one employee on cold calls and the other works on invoicing. However, that one working all the files is actually a more personable speaker, so you can switch and adapt positions based on their strengths and weaknesses.

Understanding others' emotions will help you to regulate your own as well. You will see how bad moods can affect other people, so it will be simpler for you to snap back into a good mood. You'll start to recognize what qualities you like and dislike in other notable leaders and you can either be inspired or avoid these kinds of traits.

What you have to also be aware of is how you can talk to others about their emotions. Telling someone "you seem mad," is not going to stop them from being mad. While you might be able to notice someone else's weaknesses and be aware of areas they need to work on, it is important to refrain from trying to tell them how they need to change. Let people come to some terms on their own. This is more important in your personal life, but your employees might become bothered if you are consistently giving negative feedback. When it does come time to be critical and assist with things that need to be fixed, offer up one great thing they do just as often as you would make comment on something that needs improvement.

One thing you will want to look for is the words that they are saying. Maybe they say they are "not satisfied," or that they are overly "stressed." Being stressed doesn't mean they are unhappy, but it could if they say it in a worried tone. Still, even when people say they are joking, there is going to be a morsel of truth in their words that you can understand to help you better decide which situations might need to be fixed and which are fine as they are.

Aside from their verbal language, let's take a look at how someone's body can tell us a ton about what emotional state they might be in.

# Facial Expressions and Body Language

If you have the environment with your team to do so, you should try playing games to get everyone warmed up. This can help them to be more focused and active. A great game is one that many might call charades.

Split your team in two and have each team member pretend to act out a word or phrase that the other team came up with. It can be funny and a way to loosen others up, which is especially important when many people are meeting each other for the first time. It can also be helpful in teaching your team how they can understand each other based only on their body language.

Aside from using these games to help you warm your team up, they can give you insight into how they might hold their emotions. Is someone that seems reserved really emotive when in the right context? Does the person who seems to display emotions actually have trouble trying to fake them? You can get a lot of information form a person when you see what they are like in group and game settings, especially when forced out of their comfort zone.

When reading someone's body language, start from the top of their head to the tip of their toes. There are little signals in every part of our bodies that can help let the other person know the things we might be thinking.

Look into their eyes. Are they closed? Wide? Looking somewhere else? Unfocused? How a person is holding their eyes will reveal a ton of information about the things they might be holding back. Squinted eyes might mean that they are focused, trying to really pay attention. Eyes that do not seem to be focused at all might be a sign that they are not listening to you.

Pay close attention to their brow as well. A scrunched brow might mean they are focused but pointed downwards could indicate that they are mad. Brows that are wide on their forehead could mean they are shocked, or maybe even feeling a bit anxious.

Move down to their mouth/nose area. Tight and curled lips might mean they are holding something back. An open mouth might mean that they are focused. Tight lips could mean that they are angry about something.

Blinking frequently and scattered eyesight might indicate they are nervous. They might be looking around rapidly, not able to stay concentrated on what you are saying.

If someone has trouble making eye contact with you, they could be lying, but they could also just be a really anxious person that is a little threatened by your authority. You have to really look at the context of what is being discussed if you are going to start to judge whether or not someone might be lying to you.

If they seem unfocused, they might also just be confused or maybe a little nervous about keeping up with what you are saying. Part of being emotionally intelligent will be recognizing all the ways that others could be perceiving what you are saying. When you notice all the ways your words can be interpreted, then it will be easier to assume how others might actually be reacting to your words.

Their hand over their mouth could point to the fact that they are trying to hold something back. Maybe they are struggling with taking new information in and trying to keep themselves from making any comments. They might not want you to see how they are reacting as well while they process different information.

Now, look at their arms. If they are holding them clenched and tight, they might be closed off. Crossed arms can mean that they are protecting themselves, maybe wanting to stay on the down low. Don't look too into this when you are having a casual conversation, as it sometimes just becomes a comfortable way for a person to hold their arms. At the same time, they might have done this position frequently because they are closed off, therefore it became their regular stance.

Hands on hips is just a comfortable position some sit in, but it could also have an underlying meaning. It can mean that you have authority over the room or at least are trying to take that power. You might be dominant, trying to make yourself look bigger and more easily assertive.

Notice all of this in yourself. When you really want to open up to someone, drop your arms and face yourself towards them. Keep your posture open so that they are going to be more willing to share with you as well. The more open you seem, the easier it will be for others to open up to you.

Keep your hands in sight when you want others to trust you. If you have your hands in your pocket or behind your back it can make you seem sneaky. When you are talking about big ideas, make sure that you make use of your arm movement. Make big gestures and hype up what you are talking about using articulated arm movement. Practice talking in front of the mirror so you can get an idea of how you look when giving speeches.

Make eye contact but not to the point that you are intensely staring them down. If you stare too hard into someone's eyes, it can make them feel as though you are simply intentionally trying to make them think that you are listening to them.

## Empathy Versus Sympathy

Pity is just when you simply know that someone is suffering. We can recognize when another animal is hurting and they can sometimes see when we are as well. Have you ever been around a mother and child when the mom started crying? When the baby sees the mother crying, they might start to as well. This is sometimes pity and sometimes fear that there is a greater issue at hand causing the person to be upset.

Sympathy is when you can feel sorry for someone, when you can hurt for them. We feel sympathy when people are sick or when they lose a loved one. We understand that the things they are going through are challenging and we are happy that we aren't the ones experiencing those trying times.

Empathy is when you really feel what it is like to go through what they did. Empathy is something that is hard to feel unless you have gone through a similar experience as the person that you are feeling empathetic towards. As people, we might understand what it is like to lose someone we love. It can be very heartbreaking to watch someone pass and grief can consume who we are.

Only when you are a parent; however, can you really understand what it would be like to lose a child. Only when you have lost your mother can you really know what it is like to lose a parent. Though we can relate to the people who are losing loved ones, we can really only be empathetic when we have a very deep understanding of the specific thing they are going through.

Compassion is when we will try our best to alleviate their symptoms of suffering. When you see someone hurting and you feel it is your duty to stop that pain, you are showing compassion. When you are taking care of their needs because you recognize their hurt, that is being compassionate. Most people will want to show compassion towards others, but it is less common than you'd assume. How many people do you think pass car accidents, thinking, "I hope they are OK." That's mostly empathy. Compassion is pulling over on the side of the road to really check if they are all right. You have compassion mostly for those that you care deeply for. If you saw a random car on the side of the street, you'd likely keep driving. If you noticed that car was the exact same one that your mother has, you might pull over because you are worried about her safety.

We always have to have empathy as a bare minimum for engaging with employees. We will likely have compassion but will not always have to tools necessary to alleviate that. We might want to help someone but not really have any idea how. This shows that we might still be lower on the empathy scale. If you really know what someone is suffering through, then you understand what they need to heal because you are doing what you would need in that situation to feel better. Sometimes, that simply means giving another person their space to process and heal.

There are some situations that you will not be empathetic about, but we need to do our best to try and get there. What might not sound like a big deal to you could be to your employee, so do not always base things just on your perspective. Have you ever done something scary with others and there was one person who was extra terrified? Maybe you went on a roller coaster and one friend had to get off because they were having a panic attack. Some people might call others dramatic, but that's just because they are lacking empathy. You might not be afraid of the roller coaster, but you have to understand what it might be like to be afraid of something like that and then to have to live through that fearful moment.

You need to have empathy so that you can understand how to improve the relationship overall. When you can show humility, compassion, and understanding [; that person is going to trust you so much more. They will have a way higher chance of listening to you and really believing in your mission. No one wants to invest in a robot! You will want to share that kind of humble understanding to get others to open up to you as well.

Empathy shows that you really care about that person. You are validating their experience and showing that you too are human. Again, you might not agree with why they might be feeling pain or anxiety. You might not have the same reaction to the situation. By letting that other person know you hear them, it can be all they need to feel compassion from you. This allows you to be more influential. No one wants to trust a robot!

# Important Social Skills for Interacting

You need to have a high level of emotional awareness so that your social skills will improve. Social skills are a practice. Some people might be good at them right away but for those who aren't, more emphasis needs to be placed on working to tune these right. As an entrepreneur, social skills are crucial. You can hire many people but, at the end of the day, your employees and clients will still want to hear from you. Other contractors might be able to talk to your managers that you have hired, but there will always be cases in which your input is required over all else.

Knowing whether or not you can really trust someone is very important in any business. You have to have the social skills needed to let others know that you do care about them and that they will be willing to trust you.

You have to read beyond what people tell you so that you can best determine if they are accurate candidates. Look past just the words that they are saying and see what important information you can pick up on that is hidden behind their words. Only when you do this will you be able to accurately pick out those who are most valuable to your company.

Having a high level of social perception is a skill that can enable you to really figure out what the root cause of one of your employee's performances might be. When you notice how they interact, you can start to get a sense of what they are and aren't very comfortable with. They will show more through how they interact with their coworkers and customers than they will when you are together.

You can see things you might not notice about them when you are active in watching them work. When you have meetings one on one, they will, of course, be on their best behavior. It's important to start to actually get on the floor, or in the office, or wherever your business is and work with them so that you can understand the true nature of who they are.

Once you might have identified the issues that they seem to be having and the root of what their weaknesses might be, strong social skills will be necessary so you can start to discuss a plan of improvement with them. Some people will start to get defensive if you do not approach these kinds of conversations in the right way, so you should be prepared with patient and understanding language that will help them better accept your criticism.

"Reading the room," is an important skill, especially as an entrepreneur. Sometimes, people are simply tired and you have to let them go home and start fresh the next day.

You also have to ensure that you are able to have a high level of impression management. This means that you can elicit positive emotions from your employees. They should only be inspired by you, not fearful of you. When you can motivate your team and work closely with them, it will be easier to bring out those positive moods, which means that everyone else will be much more likely to work efficiently.

Don't be afraid to flatter others. When you can throw out a compliment, people will be much more likely to respond back to you in a positive way. Don't do it in an obvious schmoozer way either; however. If you compliment a bald guy on his hair, he's going to know that you are just trying to butter him up. Look for unique flatteries that you can throw out as well. Maybe you compliment their intelligence, their ability to talk to other people, or their own personal social skills.

Hide your distaste for those around you and always be willing to give them a second chance. Even if you have met someone a couple of times and they seemed rude, you should give people a chance to warm up. You always have to be professional, of course, but never stop giving people a chance. It's always better to "kill them with kindness" instead of working off their rudeness. It'll just create an ugly cycle.

Sometimes, you might simply have to agree with others, even if it means biting your tongue. Of course, if you are making a deal, you do not want to just simply agree. However, if someone makes a comment about politics or something else that is simply opinion based, it is easier to just laugh and nod. What you say in your head you do not have to share! It's best to just try and avoid making someone upset in a business setting by trying to be combative about something that you both are entitled to your opinions on.

Persuasion is an important social skill you will want to focus on. How can you recognize someone else's viewpoint and then change it so it is more in line with what will benefit you? Persuasion is not about convincing or tricking anyone into doing something that you want them to. It's about helping them to see the perspective needed to align with yours.

Others will see their side of the story, so you have to ensure they can see your side of the story most easily. Help them realize the way that both of you can benefit when you come together and form your own perspectives and outcomes in favor of both of you.

As an entrepreneur, you need to start working on your ability to adapt to certain situations. You are a leader! You need to guide and lead the room, take it to the appropriate situation. Don't just wait for others.

Most importantly, build your communication skills so you can effectively express your ideas and visions. Keep up with your vocabulary so you know how to better form and write emails. Keep up with the news so that you have conversation starters.

Explore travel options around the world and keep up with geography so you can discuss different destinations of your clients that might be frequent travelers.

## Handling Requests from Others

You will be getting constant requests from Business Partners, Clients, Shareholders, and Subcontractors. It is important that you understand how to best handle these requests. Some of them will be easy, and others might be asking too much of you. Most will be within your job description, but others might also seem like ludicrous requests.

Of course, if you are able to do so, then do it, first and foremost. Even if it takes just a little effort on your part, small favors can go a long way. Your job as an entrepreneur, especially in the beginning, is going to be to win people over. If you have to do a little extra, then do so! Just ensure that you are properly paying your employees and compensating them for the extra work. If they get the impression that you are using their labor to promote your business without getting an extra piece of the income, then they'll lose trust in you.

When it comes to things that you can't handle, there are a few things you can do. If you feel comfortable doing so, politely decline. If not, then it is time to brainstorm an option for how to alleviate the situation. What can you tell them that's not going to upset them and still keep them on as an important customer?

Be upfront and honest about it if you can. Let's say a client asks for a custom product that's just way out of your means for completion. Perhaps it costs too much or maybe it is simply a product you do not feel comfortable making. Let them know this and then you could offer up the option to create something else.

Come up with a solution and do not give them a "yes" or "no" option. When proposing two alternatives, think of other options. Let's say someone asks for a meeting on Wednesday. That's the only day you can't do. Rather than saying, "I'm sorry, I can't do Wednesday," say something like, "Unfortunately Wednesday is not available for me, but Thursday and Friday are great."

This lets them know that a meeting, in general, is still an option, just not on their date. Remember that sometimes scheduling things can be like a ping pong match trying to find the best time for both of you. If this is occurring with an employee, it is best to reevaluate their availability and dedication to the role.

When you struggle to schedule even an interview, it is a sign they are not going to be easy to schedule for work. As far as clients go, it might be better to tell them which dates you are not available versus the ones that you are. This shows that you are more flexible and others can trust you are willing to work with them on schedules.

Let's say they ask you for something that's just way too much work to do.

Let them know this by saying, "Unfortunately I am unable to do that at the moment, but I have no problem doing this for you. If that doesn't work for you then I am also comfortable doing this."

Ask them if there is a way that you could simply help out with that need in an alternative way. As long as you are showing others that you are open to working with them, it will be a lot easier to build a solid foundation for your relationship.

At the end of the day, you simply want to ensure that they know you are not refusing because you do not want to, just that you can't.

# How to Respond to Other People's Emotions

Once you have an understanding of how to read the emotions of other people, now it is time for you to start to practice responding. The best way to respond is with a moment of silence. Never cut the person off. If they are asking a question, respond quicker. When they are explaining themselves, always give them a chance to keep going.

What you can always do to work through an emotion is to ask people questions. Wait to give advice. When you are trying to make a deal, this is when you will want to be the quietest and patient. When you aren't sure that you understand, keep asking questions. Even if you do have a good idea what they are saying, continue to ask questions to get them to reevaluate what they are saying as well. When you break apart their proposals, it gives you a chance to use influential language where needed.

People love talking about themselves and often, they just need to vent. They simply want to be heard and feel like someone cares about their feelings. When using emotional intelligence with both your employees and prospective business partners, ensure that you are giving them the grounds to talk. Never interrupt, even if you feel like what you have to say is incredibly important.

Always accept the emotion that they have. Never shame someone for being angry or upset. If you are discussing more personal things and there is a more heated moment, you will also want to make sure that people are getting their opportunity to talk.

Don't take things so personally either. If someone is frustrated with you, that doesn't mean they are questioning your character. Maybe you are telling your employees that you are unable to meet their demands and you have to turn a question they asked down. If they grow upset with you, you can't take it personally. If you do, then it can make you seem less trustworthy and they will not be as willing to open up to you down the line.

Be accommodating, no matter how ridiculous it might seem. When someone has an emotional need they really need to be met, be understanding and work with them rather than against them. If you give any indication that you are not supportive, it can quickly shut people off. They will then be more resistant in an attempt to validate their own feelings. Focus instead on finding a mutual agreement that works for everyone. When dealing with emotions, it is all about compromise.

Refrain from pointing fingers, even if they are in the wrong. Always state facts and never accuse. Even if your accusations are right, people can still be offended that you questioned their character. Be open and honest and give the other person a chance to tell their side of the story first and provide a legitimate explanation.

## How to Handle Requests When You Don't Have Time

There's seemingly never enough time for anything. When you are trying to build a successful business, you are going to be busy. It's like a newborn baby! You'd be foolish to think you could have a child without multiple sleepless nights in a row. You're going to be working well over forty hours a week in at least the first year of your business. You'd be lucky if work slows down after that! You will have to get used to turning some people's requests down when time just will not allow it.

Time is very valuable, so we can't let it slip away from us. When we let someone know we can't give them our time, we might fear they'll think we do not value them or their own time. As an emotionally intelligent entrepreneur, what's most important is that you ensure the other person that their time is still incredibly important to you, even employees.

Start by telling them that you have other commitments. Let them know it is not about who's more important, rather, what's crucial for you is that you stick to your word. You simply told someone else you could accommodate them first.

Remind them that you want time so that you can give them the best quality possible. This is especially important to remind others when you have to ask for an extension on some product or service you are providing them.

Ask them if they would be satisfied with less of your time. Not in those words, of course. If they want an hour-long dinner as a meeting, ask instead if you could meet for a quick drink. Try and simply reduce the time, not completely ignore it.

Remind them consistently you have not forgotten about them. Check in on them when you have a free moment and do your best to keep in contact even when there aren't any active business relationships. Remind them of new products and get them excited for upcoming changes.

### Explaining the Realistic Aspects of a Deadline

Some people can have some rather unrealistic explanations. People will get exciting ideas in their head and sometimes just run with that. Never make someone feel silly for having an unrealistic expectation. Simply do your best to describe why it might not be entirely possible.

First, do not be afraid to break it down for them. Be realistic. Step by step, go through the process of what they are asking and show them how things could take longer. Remind them that you respect your employees and that you have to work with them as well.

Just like you would in the last section, consistently remind your team that you are only taking the time to ensure the best quality possible. You aren't taking longer because you are lazy. You want to make it faster in the long run by ensuring there will not be any issues with quality. If you have to go back and do it again, then that'll just elongate the process.

Again, reiterate that you also have other commitments and that you are a person who sticks to their word. Remind those that are impatient that you also need to have time for things to run past when you would expect them to. In any kind of project setting, you might find that you will have issues with people running over when they say.

Give yourself a little wiggle room so you can consistently be early as well. It's better to have something early than have to apologize for having it late frequently.

### How to Motivate Your Team

Motivating your team is going to be one of the most important aspects of your job! You are like the mascot of the company. If you are uninspired, you can be certain everyone else will as well!

The best way is with rewards in monetary forms. Offer incentives for when they sell more or provide higher quality work. Give bonuses to the hardest workers. When those who excel are rewarded, it makes everyone else want to work that much harder.

That's not always in the budget, so look for other free incentives. Perhaps they have access to equipment whenever they want, as long as they sign a waiver. Let them go home early without reducing their salary, as well. Just giving them one day off could go a long way over a six-month period.

As an emotionally intelligent entrepreneur, you want to be sensitive to how people will feel personally connected to your company. Your employees will want to feel special. They want to have a purpose in your company just as you have the motives that drive the business. Without passion in your team, your business will not be as successful as it could be.

Give them a chance to grow themselves. Perhaps you do not have managerial positions, but you could offer other training that can help them further careers outside their position with you.

Have regular meetings where their voices can be heard. Don't let these meetings become useless, however! Take your team out to lunch. Make sure meetings are during business hours because if you have to take time from them, they will not be as happy.

Don't reprimand them in a way that makes them afraid. Be human when they mess up. Have discussions so that they aren't afraid to come to you when they might need help. Always be open and willing to discuss how you can work together.

# Positive and Negative Emotions in Other People

Once you have recognized these emotions and started to learn how you can sway them, now it is time to see how you can best turn those negative emotions into tools and use the positive ones as inspiration.

When your team is unhappy, it is not the end of the world. It is actually an improvement you can make for the future. When they are positive, reward this! Have an employee of the month program.

Give positive feedback on their attitudes and always remind them that they are appreciated.

### How to Handle Stress Created Outside Yourself

A lot of stress is created within ourselves, but there is certainly plenty of stress that others can create around us as well. Have someone specifically for communicative purposes if this is something that consistently stresses you out.

Have all goals for your team together so that everything stays organized. Regularly ensure that everyone knows what they need to do. Have consistent moments of de-stressing as a group. Put an emphasis on making a fun and calm environment, so that even in moments of stress, people are still going to be happy to work there.

## *Maintaining Good Relationships*

It is crucial that you start to practice how to maintain good relationships. What you will need the most is patience. Respect the way in which everyone is different and that we all operate in strange ways that others might not understand.

Always offer your ear to listen to others. The better listener you are, the more you can win over those who know you.

Be appreciative, grateful, and thankful.

Always check back in with others. At the end of the day, you need to ensure that they are feeling as though you care about them and they will, in turn, show that they care about you.

# Part 2: The 30-Day Emotional Intelligence Booster Program

The focus of these exercises is all about improving **relationships**. As an entrepreneur, it is crucial that you build relationships, as these will be the foundations of the building of your company. If everyone you interact with is one and done, then your business will not be able to fully thrive. Those you work with are people that you'll want to be coming back on a regular basis.

We will also pay special attention to the importance of **trust**. When you have trust, it will be easier to make sales and have people invest in your ideas.

**Negotiations** are key to forming good business connections. These emotional intelligence activities will help ensure that you are better prepared for meetings, discussions, and other business deals.

You will have to learn how to understand, listen, recognize, and use emotions in the right way. When you can grow these skills, it will become easier to evaluate unplanned events. You can better adjust when situations do not go as you thought they would and help to avoid any mistakes.

These thirty days provide a practical step-by-step guide to raise your EQ as an entrepreneur. This is a personally curated plan to work on your personal goals. Find something to work on that is most important to you. Pick one overall goal that you will hope to achieve at the end of this.

Perhaps you want to see an increase in employee productivity.

Maybe you want to make a big deal with potential prospects or see a jump in customer satisfaction. Whatever it is, remember that goal as you start to create smaller goals throughout each day of the upcoming month.

# Your Daily Exercise

At the end of the day, take ten minutes to do an evaluation in a personal diary. Handwritten is better, but electronic is fine as well. Writing things down will help you to remember them better. Everything we discuss should be written down in notes, so having a dedicated journal to build your EQ is going to be very helpful.

Each day, we will have a different prompt, challenge, or thought process that you will want to experience. This will happen at the end of the day as a means to help you reflect. It will only take a few moments, but you should certainly spend longer reflecting if you have the time. You will also be required to think of one emotion when you wake up, as a way to sort of get you started with the day thinking about your emotional intelligence right off the bat. Here are the steps for what you should do daily:

Step One: Right in the morning, I want to pick an emotion to recognize within yourself. I also want you to pick out what your goal at the beginning of the day will be. There is no reading required. Simply pick out one emotion that you are feeling, or maybe had felt the night before if you are still kind of groggy, and what your goal for the day is.

Step Two: At night is when you will do the reading and it will only be around ten minutes. At the end of the day, you will want to pick out that same emotion, but who else you might have seen it in. How did you recognize that person was exhibiting the emotion that you identified in the morning?

Step Three: Follow the instructions below depending on what day it is.

This is all about building relationships, so you should never just think about yourself. Look at your own thoughts and the way that you operate, but always be considerate of other people's perceptions of you as well. This is a building exercise to get you to be a more emotionally intelligent entrepreneur.

## *Day 1*

This morning, when you woke up, you should have started the daily activity of picking out one emotion that you felt. Perhaps you were feeling hopeful, angry, exhausted, annoyed, or scared. Whichever it was, that's perfectly fine! Once you finished your nightly activity of picking out the other person's emotion, it is time to do the next thing!

We will not remind you of the morning and night activities the rest of the days, so it is important that you remember throughout the month to go back and revisit these steps. Let's talk about your emotions now and how you recognize them. Perhaps you were having trouble finding the feelings within yourself. When you struggle to describe how you feel, pretend as though you are a child and you have to point to one of the frowny faces on the emotion chart. For each basic emotion that you felt, identify three more that could relate to that. Here's an example of what a journal entry would look like for today:

*"I am feeling angry, annoyed, and tired. I am feeling frustrated with what's happening, scared that the things I need to do will not get finished, and I'm sick of others not doing what they are supposed to do. I am feeling irritable like every little thing is driving me crazy. I am confused as to why it is taking people so long to finish projects. I have a short fuse because of my anger and irritability, which is likely the cause of my annoyance. I am exhausted because I feel like I am doing too much and others aren't. I feel as though I'm overworked and underappreciated. All of these emotions are basically making me feel like this as well."*

Can you see how as you start to explore those three basic emotions – anger, annoyance, and tiredness – it can help you really dig deeper to the root of the issue? From there, you can decide how to better prevent these emotions from happening the next day. Is there a clear root to this issue that you can overcome? This is something that you should be checking in on every day, but those just getting started with their emotionally intelligent journey will certainly have to practice this method of finding feelings within themselves.

## Day 2

Welcome back to day two! Congratulations for not only making it through the book but for coming back again! Though yesterday might have been simple for some, it can be incredibly challenging to figure out what your own emotions might be. Now, we are going to talk more about what it actually feels like when you are angry, sad, happy, or whatever other emotion that you might be working through. Take a look at how you're feeling today.

Do you have the same emotions that you did the night before? You can use these emotions, or you can pick out three very new ones that you felt today. Now, your goal is to recognize how these emotions feel as you are having them. What do you feel in your body? Start from the top down when doing a body scan of feelings. You can simply pick one emotion to do this with today but if you have the time, certainly do more. Here's an example of what your journal might look like:

> *"Today I was feeling pretty happy. It isn't often that I'm feeling this happy, so I want to take special note of everything that I felt so I know how to get back in this mindset again if I want to in the future.*
>
> *Starting with my head, being happy felt good. I felt a little buzz, one that kept me going even when I ran into a few annoying things that day. It helped my head out too because I didn't have those constant challenging thoughts that normally run through my mind.*
>
> *As far as the rest of my body goes, I felt good all over. At one point, my neck did hurt a little, but I was able to stretch it out and ignore it for the rest of the day. If I had been in a bad mood, I might have let this minor annoyance ruin the rest of my day. I enjoyed feeling this great and hope that I can feel like this all the time."*

Recording your emotional feelings can be helpful because you can look at the bad ones when you're in a good mood and discover a potential truth that helps you better get through them. Alternatively, you can also look at the good ones on a bad day and try to use these feelings to reverse and redirect your mood!

## Day 3

Day three and what a journey it has likely been so far! The thing about becoming emotionally intelligent is that once you do, it's hard to go back to your old ways. Even on days when you're feeling entirely terrible, you might be able to quickly pull yourself out of it because of your emotional skills. Now that you know what your emotions are and how you can try to even elicit good feelings when you're having a bad day, let's dig a little deeper.

It's time to look at the trigger of your emotions. It's important to know the difference between the cause and the trigger. You are the one that causes your emotional reaction and outside sources simply stimulate them. When you're angry, someone else might have bothered you, but you are in control of if that anger carries with you throughout the day or if you're simply able to work through it.

Pick out one emotion you had today or use one from the previous days if you didn't feel anything particularly intense today. There are three questions you need to answer to better understand the difference between feeling and intcraction. When you have determined this, it will help enlighten you as to how you can better avoid reacting the same way the next time.

What triggered the emotion you felt?

Did you react to this emotion in an appropriate way?

Was this a positive emotion that helped solve the situation?

Was this a negative emotion that made the situation worse?

Here's an example of what this journal entry might look like:

*"Today I was feeling extremely grumpy. I wasn't necessarily angry at anyone specifically; I just had a bad attitude and negative perspective.*

*This emotion ended up being triggered by the fact that I was mostly tired, had a headache, and didn't really get a good meal all day. I was just feeling pessimistic in general, mostly because I didn't feel good physically.*

*I didn't react to this appropriately. I should have been aware of my bad mood and tried to resolve it instead of spreading to others. This was not a positive emotion, but it could have been had I instead focused on making myself feel better. It was a negative emotion and it made the situation worse by putting those around me in somewhat of a bad mood as well.*

*As you can see, the emotion was triggered by these small factors that led to an even bigger mood. When you look at the root of the emotion, it becomes so much easier to figure out how you can better resolve it. If I hadn't dug deeper and question myself, then this could have turned into another bad mood the next day, only to get worse and worse if I never look deep and try to make myself feel better!"*

## Day 4

Today we are going to focus on breaking down one of the most challenging emotions one can have – anger. Look back on the past three days. How often was anger on your list of emotions? Did you mention being angry frequently throughout this time period? That's perfectly OK if so! It's time to really confront that.

Perhaps you didn't really seem angry at all before starting this but as you dug to the really deep trigger of emotion, you discovered that anger was really the root cause. We think of anger as some big muscle head with green eyes and red veins popping, yelling and punching. Anger can be rather dormant as well, hiding behind soft voices and constant nodding. Today, let's talk about anger! Answer these questions to start to break down what anger really is:

> What does it look like when you are angry?
>
> What makes you feel better when you're angry?
>
> What is something that consistently triggers your anger?
>
> What's the worst thing anger has ever caused you to do?
>
> How has anger helped you or if it never has, how can it help you in the future?

When answering these questions, it can be really helpful to actually write them down before answering, as it will reiterate the message behind the question as well. Here's an example of what this journal entry should look like:

> *"When I'm angry, I get really quiet. I rarely express myself and instead try to take some alone time. What happens because of this is that I direct that anger inwards. I become madder at myself for allowing that emotional reaction than I do to properly express anger at others who triggered it.*

*When I'm angry, it makes me feel better to talk it out. I like writing down my feelings and taking moments to reflect to really understand what caused my anger.*

*My anger is triggered when I feel stressed. If I am feeling overwhelmed, annoyed, and detached from having any fun, then I can get really angry. The worst thing anger has ever caused me to do is throw my phone at the wall when I received an email I didn't like.*

*The best thing anger caused me to do was open up to my business partner about how I felt they weren't doing their part. I told them that I was angry they weren't carrying their weight and he actually responded by saying he felt the same.*

*We realized that we just weren't working together and needed to focus on playing on each other's strengths more. It helped me to improve my relationship. When I threw my phone, it broke. This helps me realize that my anger is better used when it can build a relationship rather than break an expensive electronic."*

## Day 5

You are becoming quite the emotional expert by now and you've likely been more aware of how your moods and thoughts can really interact with your day. Let's focus more now on how these emotions will help you thrive in an entrepreneurial way.

Let's take a look back at the Ability model that we discussed when first going over EQ models of intelligence. Take each four of these aspects for measuring emotional intelligence and identify one way in which that skill will help in your specific business. When you do this, you will realize the importance of focusing on building your emotions. The four were:

> The ability to perceive emotions. This quadrant focuses on how well one can pick up on the way that others are feeling. This is also important when looking interpersonally to label your own emotions.

> Emotional Reasoning is next. This is how you are able to use your emotions for a functional purpose.

> The next is understanding emotions. How well are you able to really see the root of the emotion.

> The next is the management of emotions. Can you control how you might react to any given stimuli?

Now, identify a way that each of these can help your specific business. Include your vision so that you better understand why it's important for you, not just entrepreneurs in general.

Here is an example of what a journal entry might look like:

> *"The ability to perceive emotions is going to help me at my coffee shop. When I can tell if my employees are happy or unhappy, I can better determine if the position they are in is the right one for them.*

> *Emotional reasoning is important because when I'm feeling like others might not be performing to the best of their ability, I can communicate this effectively in a way that keeps everyone focused and working.*

> *Understanding emotions is important because when an employee comes to me with a problem, I will be able*

*to see the root of what they're saying as well as, the deeper issue that they might not even be aware of themselves.*

*Managing emotions is important for myself because I want my employees to respect me and be happy. It's important for me to know how to alleviate certain moods because it will help me be a better manager and leader to the rest."*

## Day 6

Welcome to day six! You have almost completed a week, and that is something to be immeasurably proud of. It is never easy to have to look inside yourself to see what's really going on.

When we're completely unaware of our emotions, it can cause us to end up being really destructive with them. Let's revisit another model for this activity. Refer back to the mixed model. Today, use each of those sections of the Mixed Model to identify how unregulated emotions within that category might lead to negative outcomes or how unrecognized emotions could cause a bigger issue. These are the five categories:

**Self-Awareness:** What's an emotion that if you are not aware of, could cause issues in your business? How could being not-self-aware cause a problem?

**Self-Regulation:** If you fail to regulate yourself, what damage could this cause your company?

**Motivation:** Why is motivation necessary for your company? Who is it that needs motivated?

**Empathy:** What good will empathy do in your company?

**Social Skills:** What could potentially happen if you do not have a high level of social skills in your business?

Now, answer these questions, and really understand why each of these measurements for EQ are important in order to keep your emotional intelligence in check. Here's what a journal entry for this day might look like:

> *"When I'm not aware of my anger, it can put me in a really bad mood. This could bleed into the moods of my employees at my writing company, so I need to ensure everyone is in a good mood so that we have a high quality of content consistently coming out. If I do not regulate my feelings and actively try to seek out the things that feel good, then I won't be able to recognize these feelings and use them in productive and healthy ways. I need to motivate myself to do better, but I also need to motivate my team, so they consistently come out with high-quality content that drives sales even further. I need empathy so that I can be understanding to their needs. If I show them empathy, then they'll show me respect and this is what a good working environment is all about. Most important are my social skills so that I can better talk about issues and communicate the things that I am wanting from my employees."*

### Day 7

Wow! It's the end of the first week and things are probably looking great for you! It can feel really great to fully identify all the things that we need to work on and how we might have been struggling in the past. You are likely feeling enlightened and inspired. Perhaps your confidence level has boosted or you've already noticed a way that you and a friend or colleague are working on your relationship.

For this day, we are going to work on identifying how our emotional intelligence has now become a personality trait. When you really open up the door of your emotions and start facing them for what they are, then you will be able to start to better recognize all the ways that they have changed your life for the better.

In the trait model, it explores the idea that you are an emotionally intelligent person and that those personality traits can either be hidden or flourished. It's not about learning a new skill like you might if you want to skateboard or play the violin. It's a skill that already exists inside of you and you can form your personality to align with this.

Let emotional intelligence be a part of you, not the skill that you do. For this activity, rate each thing in two different ways. The first one, rate what you would say about yourself and the second, rate for what you would think others would answer for you. To keep score, 1 means completely agree and 5 means completely disagree.

1. When you are presented with a very attractive offer, you go for it right away.

2. When someone has a problem with you and starts to pick a fight, you get defensive and start to argue right back.

3. When you feel like you need to say what's on your mind, it's easier for you to bite your tongue than to try and speak up.

4. It is hard for you to really relate to other people. You have trouble seeing their pain and even think some people might be acting dramatically.

5. When you are stressed, it's hard for you to control those feelings.

If you want, you can even ask someone else to rate these for you. Then, add up your score out of 25 possible points and add it together with your score for how you think others would perceive you.

For example, you might think that you completely disagree with all of these things, but a friend would say that you are somewhere in the middle. Your score was 25 and theirs for you was 15. Add those together and then times by two. This will be your percentage out of 100. This would give me 80 percent, which isn't bad but I would need to work on how others perceive me and the way that I might express some of my emotions

Anything above 75 percent is good, but you should really be working towards getting all fives, where you completely disagree with the statements above. This is the last time that we'll be going over examples for journal entries or what the outcome of these readings might look like.

Now, it is time to move onto week two, where the daily discussions will be more focused on reflecting and writing rather than reading! The entries will be shorter, which means you'll need to spend more time writing. Ensure that you're not forgetting to do your daily morning and night exercises of identifying one emotion either. This will be very important in your continued practice of increased emotional intelligence.

## *Day 8*

For today's activity, you will want to identify one emotion that you've had in the past. This emotion should come from the past week and it should be one that we would refer to as more challenging. Maybe you think of it in a negative light, but this activity is going to be all about how you can turn that negative emotion into the positive one. If for some amazing reason you had no negative emotions at all whatsoever last week, then look to a different time in your past where you experienced a negative emotion.

This emotion is one that felt bad to have – anger, grief, jealousy, rage, and so on. Here is what you will want to write about in your journal. Answer these questions and elaborate for more than ten minutes if you have the time. If not, giving yourself a minimum of five minutes to reflect will do as well:

What was the challenging emotion and the trigger/events leading up to it?

How did it negatively affect you, increase your emotions, or even affect others around you?

If you had a time machine and could go back to this moment, how could you have used that negative emotion for something good?

## *Day 9*

A lot of times, it can be easier to simply repress our emotions than trying to have to work through them. This is never going to do you any good, however! Going forward, what you'll want to focus on is finding a balance between expression and repression, while doing your best to not worry about and freak out to your emotions.

For today's activity, it's important that you find three methods in which you can fully express yourself. To do this, start by looking at a way that you can express yourself when you're angry at yourself. Perhaps writing helps, going for a jog, or zoning out and playing a game. This isn't about pushing those feelings down but letting yourself be angry and work through them.

Your second method should be one that you can use with others. How can you properly express to someone that you are feeling bad? Maybe there is a word that you can use to let someone else know that you're feeling triggered or perhaps you have a specified room you go to when you're upset to use as a signal for others when you're angry. This second method is all about alleviating anger in relationships.

The third method is one that you should use to instantly alleviate your feelings. Perhaps it is a breathing technique, such as counting down from ten. Maybe it's a song that you can play that will instantly make you feel better. The third one should be focused on something that gives instant relief.

To recap, these are the things you need to come up with:

1. A way to relieve negative emotions within yourself.

2. A way to express negative emotions to others in a healthy way.

3. A way to instantly relieve negative emotions.

## *Day 10*

This week, we are going to put an emphasis on making sure that you know how to take some time before reacting. It can be hard to not just say the first thing that comes to your mind. When you do this; however, you're putting yourself at risk for saying something that you don't mean. Our reactions can really cause bigger issues if we're not careful.

To practice this, I want you to think of a time that someone said something rude to you or a moment when you were really upset. What's a comment that someone else shared that really stuck with you? If you have trouble thinking of this, try and imagine what an insecurity you have might be and a comment someone might make based on that.

From there, I want you to come up with three responses. Your first one is instant, right away. Right it down without even thinking about it. Then, I want you to really think about an appropriate response. Once that is done, then tomorrow, come back and think of your third response. You don't have to write it down, but it will help you to look back on these responses and think of something more articulated and different from the first response. This activity will help you to start to see how reacting impulsively isn't always the best option.

## Day 11

Tonight, make sure that you peek back at yesterday's journal to see your responses. Once you have done that, along with your other daily activities, we're going to focus now on how to recognize the emotions and feelings of other people.

Look back in your journal and go through and refresh yourself on the one emotion that you've been noticing in others every day in the past. For all of those people whose emotions you recognized, I want you to point out one strength and one weakness they have.

Once you have done this, then you should look back and reflect on those emotions and see if there is anything that might connect their emotion to their strengths/weaknesses. Is there something they could improve on? If these are your employees and you've noticed a pattern in their mood and their performance, then can you come up with a solution to resolve any negative feelings? This activity will help you start to see the correlation between emotion and behavior in other people.

## Day 12

Today's activity might be something a little more challenging. I want you to think of someone that you aren't particularly a fan of. It could be someone you see on a regular basis – perhaps a client that's very difficult or even your spouse's sibling! If you struggle to think of someone you don't like, maybe you even consider a celebrity or notable figure that you just aren't very interested in. Whoever this is, I want you to really put yourself in their shoes. I don't want you to just think of this as them now – look back throughout their entire lives.

If you start to realize that there's a lot that you don't know about them, where they came from, how they were raised, or the experiences they went through, then perhaps there's something about them that you just don't really know. Maybe this is enough to have you reconsider why you don't like them in the first place! The point of this activity is to help you see why someone else might feel the way they do. You don't have to entirely agree with their behavior, but walking farther than just a mile through someone's life can be enough to help you see connections you might not have noticed the first time around.

## Day 13

Remember that person we had you thinking about yesterday? You can do this activity with the same person in mind, but if you want to avoid thinking about them or just expand to someone else, that's fine for this part too. What you will want to do today is look at that person's triggers. What is it that might set someone off? What about a person could put them in a bad mood? Maybe the person you chose to focus on is someone that you dislike because they're so rude to you.

Look at the root of this – what happened in their life to make them feel that way?

When you can start to understand this, it will become much easier for you to "deal" with them or at least not be so upset when they're mad at you. When we dislike others, we think of them as how they're treating us. Remember that they have their own perspectives as well and each thing will give you insight into why they might act a certain way. This activity will help you see how even though you don't agree with their behavior, you can still be empathetic towards their actions.

## Day 14

Welcome back! You've almost made it half-way through the readings! For today, we are going to focus again on understanding someone else. Rather than looking at someone you dislike, we're going to focus on someone that has hurt you in the past. Whether it was from your high school days or someone that really hurt you last week, pick out someone that has caused you emotional pain. Forgiving can be hard, but something you have to do not for them, but for you.

Now, let's look at the same things we have the past three days, but for them. Answer these questions in your journal.

> What emotions and feelings do you think they had around the time they caused the hurt?

> Why do you think they were OK with inflicting pain on someone else?

> Where did their emotions come from? What was their trigger?

> Why did they act, say things, or speak in the way they did that hurt you?

When you start to really break down someone else's actions, it becomes so much easier to see that they weren't always hurting you because of something wrong with you. As an emotionally intelligent person, you're going to need to focus on how hurt people can often end up hurting other people.

## Day 15

There are plenty of useful and healthy ways that you are going to be able to use your emotions in different negotiations. The key is that you have control over these emotions. If you don't then that can hinder your ability to actually make a deal. Right now, I want you to identify three basic emotions that you often feel when making negotiations.

Then, you will want to identify one way that you can turn these emotions into something different. For example, anxiety can turn into passion if directed in a healthy way. Anger can be motivation. Make a list of these three emotions and turn them into something positive.

Then, I want you to look at the way that this will be able to help you better make negotiations. Identify the ways that the negative emotions are going to help you get people to trust you more and how you can close deals when you turn the good into bad. If you have time, try your best to find more than one emotion to change.

## Day 16

You've officially made it halfway through this book and that's something that we all need to take a moment and be proud of. It's never easy to look deep inside who you are and start to pick apart the things that you might or might not like about yourself. You've done that so far!

The next step, after you recognize and understand what your emotions are, is to look where the feelings come from. Naturally, as you begin to question your motives, you've likely already thought of this. Now; however, it's time to really look at the root cause of your emotions.

For this activity, you are going to write a brief biography of who you are, using bullet points.

Start with the very moment you were born and work up to where you are now. Split these bullet points into two categories. One category is going to be good and one category bad. For memories that you don't like, things that are a little more tragic, maybe a death, an accident, a sickness, or something else that wasn't pleasant to live through, put that in one section. Then the good things, maybe a move, a new job, a baby, and other happy things, put that in one category. If you don't have time to go through everything, this will bleed into tomorrow's entry as well!

## *Day 17*

For today's entry, let's ensure that you've finished your biography first. It shouldn't be too extensive; you're really just categorizing events. Now, look at those negative times and see if there are things from them that you haven't recovered from. Do you hold onto trauma from an accident? Are there still hurt feelings from a break-up? When you see that there are leftover feelings, you well better realize that you have emotions that still play into who you are today. For today's journal entry, write about what things from your past still affect the way you feel on a consistent basis.

## Day 18

A huge part of maintaining healthy relationships is reacting to the way others speak and listening to them with a higher skill level. We often don't listen to others very well, or when we do listen, we might react in a way that makes them afraid to talk to us.

One way to practice your listening skills and increase the way you react is to watch more speeches online. For this activity, find a speech of someone on YouTube in a topic of interest. One pertaining to entrepreneurial skills you need to increase would probably be the best choice! Now, instead of listening to it at regular speed, increase it by two and see if you can really pick up on what they're saying.

Then, watch it through a second time at regular length, ensuring that you pay attention to every word they say. Take notes on what you learned immediately after. Each time you notice yourself losing interest and not focusing, make sure to redirect attention immediately. The purpose of this activity is to help you understand the difference between listening to the words someone is saying and the meaning of what they said overall.

## Day 19

This activity is one that we're taking you outside of your journal to do! If you have already opened up to someone about this challenge, then that is great and you should choose them as they'll be understanding of this activity. If not, find someone that you feel really close with. Ask them how they are doing and really get them to open up.

Ask questions to keep them going and always repeat back what they said if you want to reiterate one of their points. This activity is to help you better listen. The challenge will be to not mention anything about yourself and to only have the attention on the other person. Think of it like you're interviewing a best friend! They'll have fun sharing their story and they'll appreciate the set of ears you have to listen!

## *Day 20*

You are someone that's becoming quite the emotional genius! You know how to recognize your own emotions, pick up on others, and show empathy to allow others to feel more connected to you. How is your stress level, however?

For today's journal entry, you are going to want to identify the top five things that have been stressing you out. Once you have identified these, come up with a plan to reduce the stress. Is it something you can cut out, or cut down time spent on it? Is it something that you have to do a stress-relieving activity afterward? Tonight, focus on identifying your stressors and coming up with ways to alleviate them.

## *Day 21*

Now that you're nice and relaxed, no longer as stressed, let's focus on something that might be keeping you still high-strung – complaining. As you're becoming more emotionally intelligent, it can be difficult to deal with others who are constantly complaining. Whether it's a customer, an employee, or even your business partner, we might notice others suffering by their own hands as we're becoming more self-aware.

Refrain from preaching to others about emotional intelligence. What you have to do is show that you are hearing the other person's suffering and you are willing to come up with a plan to help them with their complaint. For tonight's journal entry, think of the top three complaints you hear. Then, craft two responses to each that you can use next time someone comes to you with a complaint.

## Day 22

The key to productivity is having an environment that not only enables that but encourages it. If you want your employees to give you the results you want, then you have to ensure that your working environment is one that they are comfortable in. For this activity, you are going to come up with a plan for creating a work environment. The keys will be:

1. Comfortability

2. Communication

3. Calming environment

Are your employees comfortable? Do they have a nice restroom to use, snacks available, a fridge to keep their food? You'll want your employees to feel at home. Next, consider your communication policies. Can they come to you whenever they want to talk? Do you have an anonymous way to report any serious issues? Finally, consider the overall aesthetic of your office or work environment. Consider having art, using some plants, or changing up the lighting to make it a place that people really feel inspired to work.

## Day 23

For this activity, we are going to focus solely on giving the correct guidance. If you want to be the type of leader that people look up to and want to really work for, then you have to know how to provide them with quality advice and beneficial direction for both you and them.

For this journal entry, write about a small issue that you have in your life, but not one that you can't figure out how to fix. Maybe a friend is mad at you, you have a bill overdue, you have high blood pressure, or you need to buy a new appliance.

In your journal, also write a way to solve this problem. Write the solution to yourself. Let yourself be the guider. When you do this, you enable yourself to see how your advice might sound to others. Do you give advice that is just based on the easiest and most obvious solution or do you give guidance based on what works for the individual in their specific scenario?

## Day 24

Throughout this thirty-day journey, you have likely grown immensely in your abilities as an emotionally intelligent being. Though this is true, there's a good chance that you've still had some moments where you let your emotions get the best of you. For your journal entry, look back on the past couple of weeks and pick out a moment that you were angry. Then, you will want to identify how that anger helped you. How were you able to push through it and use it for good?

After that, ask yourself these questions. When is it OK to get angry? What does your healthy anger look like? What is the way to get angry in a civilized and productive way? When you can pick these out, it becomes much easier to see the benefits of anger. Compare your anger reactions now, to how they might have looked when you first started this thirty-day challenge.

## *Day 25*

The most important part of this all was to help you build on your relationships! For this journal entry, you are going to want to identify the most important kinds of relationships you have. What matters to you the most? Pick out the most important business relationships, your employee relationships, your clients, and everyone else pertaining to your relationship.

Pick out what you have to offer them and what they have to offer you. Decide if this is a fair amount being provided between the both of you. Is this something that needs to grow? Are you doing your part? Do you feel as though they are providing their part as well? When you pick this out, it becomes easier to see the strengths and weaknesses in your most valuable relationships.

## Day 26

In order to maintain those strong relationships, you'll need to put an emphasis on the most important interactions between you and these other people. Preparing for important meetings, discussions, and negotiations are important. For this activity, you are going to want to draft up a preparation checklist. This is good for your emotional intelligence because it gives you something to look at each and every time you have one of these meetings and ensure that you are prepared. The things you might include would be:

1. Ensuring your speech is prepared.

2. Making sure everyone knows what is going to be discussed in the meeting.

3. Coming up with responses – more than one option for each potential response.

Your checklist will look different, but this will give you something to alleviate anxiety so that you can know you'll be prepared for each meeting.

## Day 27

The time is almost here for your thirty-day challenge to be over! You are probably feeling so much better than at the start. You have the ability to recognize your emotions and come up with your own healthy ways of working through them! Not only that, but you are able to better pick out exactly what's wrong and how to fix the problem.

One important thing to remember is going to be how you can prepare for unplanned events. As an emotionally intelligent person, you have to learn the line between being realistically prepared for something and anxious or scared over when it will happen. For this activity, write a letter to your past-self. Remind the old you that everything has worked out fine so far.

Of course, there are times that you might have wanted a better outcome, but everything that's occurred has unfolded just as it was supposed to. Share your biggest fears, your biggest pieces of advice, and the things that you wish you knew. When you're done, read it over again and remind yourself of how this will help you live happily now. Of course, you'll always want to be prepared for some of the crazy things life has to offer, but at the end of the day, you can never be too worried or scared about what the future holds or else you'll miss out on what's happening around you now!

## Day 28

Only three days left! For this day, I want you to come up with your own test in order to find your emotional intelligence score using the ability model. Come up with around five questions per category. They can be small questions, nothing that requires too much response.

Give yourself the test to see how you have really grown throughout this process. Ask someone else to score you as well, to see if the perceptions others have of you has changed at all as well. You could even use this test to interview potential candidates in the future!

## Day 29

It's the second to last day and you're probably feeling pretty confident with your emotions. As another review, let's look back at the mixed model to judge emotional intelligence. For this, come up with yet another test to score your emotional intelligence.

The grading skill for this one could be something like choosing from 1 to 5 on how much you agree/disagree like the one we did earlier. Test yourself and go ahead and test someone else as well to see what they think. Maybe you do this in a business meeting or team meeting for your employees. Get a sense of the things that both you and others might still have to work on together.

## Day 30

Wow! The last day! It's really inspiring to feel this way, as an emotionally intelligent entrepreneur. This entry is going to be the longest of all. I want you to start by using the trait model of emotional intelligence and think of how this is now your personality. What personality traits do you carry now that help point out your level of emotional intelligence?

Identify the ways that you have changed and how you have grown because of this experience. Compare your newest entries to even the ones that you started with.

Going forward, we encourage you to take this challenge again, as it will only help you get to an even deeper level of your emotions! Share with others, especially those in your business, to help others improve. Remember that this isn't the end –

this is the start of an inspiring journey for you and your business.

# Independent author

As an independent author,
   and one-man operation
   - my marketing budget is next to zero.

As such, the only way
   I can get my books in-front of valued customers
   is with reviews.

Unfortunately, I'm competing against authors and
   giant publishing companies
   with multi-million-dollar marketing teams.

These behemoths can afford
   to give away hundreds of free books
   to boost their ranking and success.

Which as much as I'd love to –
   I simply can't afford to do.

That's why your honest review
   will not only be invaluable to me,
      **but also to other readers on Amazon**.

Yours sincerely,

Joel E. Winston

# Further reading

Standing still is going backwards. If you have enjoyed this book and you want to keep improving your results and income as an Entrepreneur, check out the following title from the same author.

*Stoicism for Entrepreneurs*
*How to model todays best entrepreneurs by using the ancient stoic self-disciplined mindset*
*Joel E. Winston*

Here is a tiny bit of what you´ll discover:

- **How to persevere even if the odds seem stacked against you** (page 61)
- How to deal with the obstacles you face as an entrepreneur (page 42)
- One simple rule to help you decide where to put your energy and focus (page 60)
- How to raise your Self-Confidence as an entrepreneur (page 65)
- The No.1 method for continuous self-improvement in only 20 minutes a day (page 23)
- How to *increase your entrepreneurial motivation* and get more done in less time (page 57)
- To stoic way of turning adversity and setbacks into growth and improvements (page 59)
- How to **improve the relationship with your business partners** and get more business (page 70 and 82)
- How a holistic approach on life will benefit your business (page 83)

And much, much more.

Don´t waste your time and get more productive and learn how to deal with obstacles.

Go to Amazon and search for: ´Stoicism for Entrepreneurs´

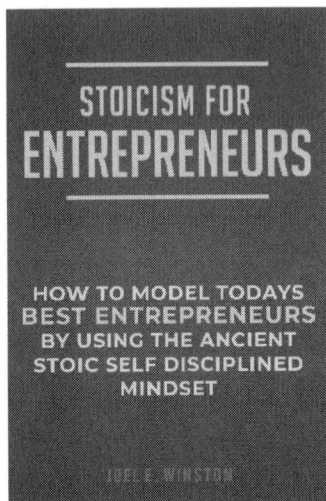

If you feel like you don´t have enough time to read, I have great news. You can listen to the audio version of this book for **FREE**, by signing up for FREE for the 30-day audible trail.

You can cancel the trial any time for any reason.

Audible Trial Benefits:

- **FREE audio copy** of this book

- After, the free trail, you will get 1 credit per month to use on any audiobook available.

- Choose from Audible´s 200,000 + titles

- Listen anywhere with the Audible app across multiple devices

- If you don´t love an audiobook, exchange easy for another one without hassle

- You will keep your audiobooks forever, even if your cancel your membership

And much, much more

Click on one of the below links and start listening for FREE to this $14,95 audiobook.

Link to listen for free on Audible US:
https://adbl.co/2wQsTp6

Link to listen for free on Audible UK:
https://adbl.co/2R742Xu

Link to listen for free on Audible FR:
http://bit.ly/2X4UQZ5

Link to listen for free on Audible DE:
https://adbl.co/2I8rOQo

**Your audiobook is waiting...**

STOICISM FOR
ENTREPRENEURS

HOW TO MODEL TODAYS
BEST ENTREPRENEURS
BY USING THE ANCIENT
STOIC SELF DISCIPLINED
MINDSET

**Stoicism for Entrepreneurs**
How to Model Todays Best Entrepreneurs by Using the Ancient Stoic Self Disciplined Mindset

By: Joel. E. Winston
Narrated by: Seth Thompson
Length: 3 hrs and 15 mins
★ ★ ★ ★ ★ 5.0 (25 ratings)

Free with 30-day trial

$14.95/month after 30 days. Cancel anytime.

Or, Buy for $14.95

▶ Sample

# References

Cherry, K. (2019). The 6 Types of Basic Emotions and Their Effect on Human Behavior. Retrieved from https://www.verywellmind.com/an-overview-of-the-types-of-emotions-4163976

Donaldson, M. (2019). Plutchik's Wheel of Emotions - 2017 Update • Six Seconds. Retrieved from https://www.6seconds.org/2017/04/27/plutchiks-model-of-emotions/

Goleman, Daniel. Emotional Intelligence: Why It Can Matter More Than Iq. New York: Bantam Books, 1995. Print.

Levine, M. (2019). Logic and Emotion. Retrieved from https://www.psychologytoday.com/us/blog/the-divided-mind/201207/logic-and-emotion

Salovey, P., Brackett, M., & Mayer, J. (2007). Emotional intelligence. Port Chester, N.Y.: Dude Pub.

Srivastava K. (2013). Emotional intelligence and organizational effectiveness. Industrial psychiatry journal, 22(2), 97–99. doi:10.4103/0972-6748.132912

Stosny, S. (2019). The Function of Emotions. Retrieved from https://www.psychologytoday.com/us/blog/anger-in-the-age-entitlement/201612/the-function-emotions

26614571R00076